PRAISE FOR *THE BOOK OF AWESOME BLACK WOMEN*

"Formidable and daring, resilient and hopeful, *The Book of Awesome Black Women* is a beacon of acknowledgment for the transformative work Black women have done and continue to do. Rendered with simple truth and trailblazing candor, we are honored by their lives, their stories, their grace and the inspirational precedent set for all to follow in their footsteps."

—**Bridgitte Jackson-Buckley**, interviewer, memoirist, and author of *The Gift of Crisis: How I Used Meditation to Go From Financial Failure to a Life of Purpose*

"In *The Book of Awesome Black Women*, Becca Anderson and M.J. Fievre remind us how central Black women are and have been to American and world history and culture. No matter how much you think you know about the awesomeness of Black women, this book will give you more reasons to celebrate what Black women have done and are destined to do. This book is a balm and a healing for all who will read it."

—**Marita Golden**, author of *The Strong Black Woman: How a Myth Endangers the Physical and Mental Health of Black Women*

"*The Book of Awesome Black Women* is a powerful resource for young Black girls to empower themselves with the stories of their foremothers. The Black women in this book will guide and lead future generations to recognize that they have the love, strength, and ferocity to change their world."

—**Karen Arrington**, author of *Your Next Level Life: 7 Rules of Power, Confidence, and Opportunity for Black Women in America*

"*The Book of Awesome Black Women* is full of Black women trailblazers who have paved the way for future generations of Black girls to build their own achievements, successes, and triumphs. Here are the foremothers whose stories and lives will help teach young Black girls the power they hold within to change and redefine social boundaries."

—**Varla Ventura**, author of S*heroes: Bold, Brash, and Absolutely Unabashed Superwomen*

"A celebration of indomitable Black women who scaled centuries of oppression to reach the mountaintop. The encapsulated biographies prove that the impossible can be possible."

—**Marlene Wagman-Geller**, author of *Women of Means: The Fascinating Biographies of Royals, Heiresses, Eccentrics and Other Poor Little Rich Girls*

"The world needs more works celebrating the excellence of strong, accomplished Black women! This is an excellent introduction to those who've earned their places in history."

—**Chrisanne Beckner**, architectural historian, writer, and author of *100 African Americans Who Shaped American History*

THE
BOOK OF
AWESOME
BLACK
WOMEN

OTHER BOOKS BY BECCA ANDERSON

Badass Affirmations

The Book of Awesome Women

The Book of Awesome Girls

The Book of Awesome Women Writers

Badass Women Give the Best Advice

You Are an Awesome Woman

Think Happy to Stay Happy

The Woman's Book of Prayer

Let Me Count the Ways

The Joy of Self-Care

The Crafty Gardener

Every Day Thankful

I Can Do Anything

OTHER BOOKS BY M.J. FIEVRE

*Badass Black Girl: Quotes, Questions, and
Affirmations for Teens*

*Empowered Black Girl: Joyful Affirmations and Words
of Resilience*

*Black and Resilient: 52 Weeks of Anti-Racist Activities for
Black Joy & Resilience*

*Resilient Black Girl: 52 Weeks of Anti-Racist Activities for Black
Joy & Resilience*

*Happy, Okay? Poems about Anxiety, Depression, Hope
and Survival*

*Raising Confident Black Kids: A Comprehensive Guide for
Empowering Parents and Teachers of Black Children*

Young Trailblazers: The Book of Black Inventors and Scientists

*Young Trailblazers: The Book of Black Heroes
and Groundbreakers*

Walk Boldly: Empowerment Toolkit for Young Black Men

THE BOOK OF AWESOME BLACK WOMEN

Sheroes, Boundary Breakers,
and Females who Changed the World

M.J. FIEVRE
& BECCA ANDERSON

mango
PUBLISHING GROUP
CORAL GABLES

For permission requests, please contact the publisher at:
Mango Publishing Group
2850 S Douglas Road, 4th Floor
Coral Gables, FL 33134 USA
info@mango.bz

For special orders, quantity sales, course adoptions and corporate sales, please email the publisher at sales@mango.bz. For trade and wholesale sales, please contact Ingram Publisher Services at customer.service@ingramcontent.com or +1.800.509.4887.

The Book of Awesome Black Women: Sheroes, Boundary Breakers, and Females who Changed the World

Library of Congress Cataloging-in-Publication number: 2022933220
ISBN: (p) 978-1-64250-929-8 (e) 978-1-64250-930-4
BISAC category code YAN006140, YOUNG ADULT NONFICTION / Biography & Autobiography / Women

Printed in the United States of America

Contents

Preface

"The most disrespected person in America is
the Black woman.

The most unprotected person in America is the
Black woman.

The most neglected person in America is the
Black woman."

—Malcolm X, 1962

E very few years, to prove itself post-racial, America goes
through waves of revolution, promises change at every
turn, and then goes back to *business as usual*. This time
around, however, things feel a bit different in the land of
the free: we are on the edge of a new dawn. America sees
through the veil of racism, even if it still must work harder
to lift it completely. And the gauge of success for a new
America that overcomes racial inequality and injustice will
undoubtedly have to be Black women.

Malcolm X was correct in his assessment of Black women's
condition: Black women are systematically sidelined,

neglected, and discriminated against, and they carry the
stigma of being both Black and female, which means
they stand at the crossroad of racism and sexism, facing
misogynoir.[1] Be it in the boardroom, the classroom, the
athletic arena, or anywhere in between, Black women end
up with the short end of the proverbial stick, relegated to
the back hallways and waiting rooms or offered a voiceless
seat at the table so that the powers that be may fulfill efforts
of feigned inclusion. In the field of healthcare alone, Black
women's pain is consistently overlooked and undermanaged.
Black mothers are the most at risk, and Black babies face
a higher mortality rate. When young Black men die or are
incarcerated in disproportionate numbers, their Black female
counterparts are left alone to deal with the fallout, and yet
Black women are still expected to pull through and hold their
communities and families together.

In the last couple of years, we have opened our eyes to
how Black women consistently and competently show up,
excel, and exceed standard expectations. This "leveling
up," of course, is not a new phenomenon. This is what we do
and have done throughout history. From Harriet Tubman,
Fannie Lou Hamer, and Shirley Chisholm to Oprah Winfrey,
Michelle Obama, Misty Copeland, and Simone Biles, we
have always written our names in the stars the way our
ancestors dreamed. Black women's accomplishments are
noteworthy and deserving of praise. Unlike women of other
races, Black women have had to work and fight harder for
their achievements, and even when they do reach success,
they often fail to be recognized as anything but "less than."

• • • • •

1   a term coined by scholar Kimberlé Crenshaw

And there is a generation of Black girls growing up right now who need role models in their lives who look like them, because these girls will face—or already face—the same kind of discrimination their foremothers did.

In this book, we have documented a treasure trove of brilliant and stellar Black women who have paved the way for the modern generation of Black girls and continue to do so with impenetrable tenacity, valiant willpower, and relentless ambition. Now, more than ever, is the time to crash through glass ceilings and triumph over tribulations that persist with the plight of Black people. As Black women are stepping into roles that were previously closed off to them, becoming vice president, decorated gymnasts, accomplished scientists, thinkers, researchers, activists, agents of change, and more, we are adding our voices to the conversation, with this book as our contribution. *The Book of Awesome Black Women* is the product of two minds in publishing and women's empowerment, both of them authors who are more than familiar with female trailblazers breaking boundaries. Becca Anderson (author of *The Book of Awesome Women* and *The Book of Awesome Girls*) and I, M.J. Fievre (author of the Badass Black Girl series and the Young Trailblazers series), have combined our efforts with one single goal: reaching into the past to look at the Black women who came before us, who laid the foundation for today, and who are still doing the work.

In *The Book of Awesome Black Women,* you'll find stories of women who broke the chains that bound them. You'll find women who, despite the odds stacked against them, managed to succeed and thrive, and you'll find women who built on the successes of their foremothers and innovated technology, entertainment, and the world at large. These women deserve to be celebrated for their remarkable successes and achievements. These are unstoppable women with lessons to teach about persistence. We want to provide our readers with various role models and inspiration to guide them into stepping out into the world, no matter what they choose to do or who they choose to be. We hope you'll enjoy reading about the awesome Black women as much as we enjoyed discovering their stories.

The time for Black women to be praised and recognized for their power is now. That moment is in fact overdue, and books like this one must come from a place of love and intention and from the hard work of authors who aim to honor Black women, researching the most important resources for our readers. This is the right time for a book like this to take its place in a canon that has consistently sought to erase our accomplishments and our names from history. We stake our claim on this moment as ours to redress these wrongs and open the doors for the rest of us waiting our turn to come through and take our seat at the table.

M.J. Fievre, author of the Badass Black Girl series

Introduction

All women have the same maternal ancestor, and she was a Black woman from Africa two hundred thousand years ago. This "mitochondrial Eve" has passed down her unique genetic code, her mitochondrial DNA, from woman to woman, so in a way, she is the mother of all humankind, and every awesome Black woman in this book is her daughter.

One of her most fearless daughters was the beloved Audre Lorde, who in turn was the mother of intersectional feminism. Lorde fought to educate those in the public and in academia that womanhood, race, and sexuality are inseparable, that they inform one another, and that their interconnectedness deserves to take up space. She also advocated for the collaboration of women with different identities, for within those differences and that collaboration lay the key to their creation of liberation from the oppression of the patriarchy. In her famous 1984 speech "The Master's Tools Will Never Dismantle the Master's House," Lorde states that:

> "[T]hose of us who stand outside the circle of this society's definition of acceptable women; those of us who have been forged in the crucibles of difference—those of us who are poor, who are lesbians, who are Black, who are older—know that survival is not an academic skill. It is learning how to take our differences and make them strengths."

Throughout this book, you will find multifaceted women who were friends, contemporaries, and mentors to each other, who acted in the spirit of Lorde's vision for the liberation of women, and who chose to empower rather than trample one another.

In these pages, you will discover some exemplars of awesome Black women who uplifted each other, such as Lucy Terry Prince, a Black slave whose poetry was orally passed down by fellow slaves in colonial America. Think about that for a minute: Prince was denied agency, yet she pursued her creativity fully and generously by sharing her talents for writing and oration with other Black women.

There Is so much women's history yet to be uncovered and explored, and that is especially true of Black women's history.

Katherine Johnson, who was nicknamed the "human computer" by her male colleagues at NASA, is largely responsible for the mathematical engineering and underpinnings which helped humankind reach the moon. She should have been a household name for that accomplishment alone, but it was only when she and her cohort were featured in the book and film *Hidden Figures* that most of the world outside of NASA learned about her brilliance and oh-so important work.

Harriet Tubman may be famous for her work associated with freeing slaves through the Underground Railroad, but her impact on history is even bigger than that, if one can believe it. Not only was she a "conductor" of the Underground Railroad, she was also a spy, guerrilla soldier, and nurse for the Union army during the Civil War. She is even considered the first Black woman to serve in the military. From an early age, Harriet had an unstoppable spirit, one that prevailed against violence. When she was twelve, she was struck on the head by her master for intervening in the beating of an enslaved man who tried to escape. Because of this attack, she suffered from narcolepsy, yet she continued with her serious abolition work as well as her women's suffrage work. Harriet was a multidimensional woman whose fighting spirit freed countless souls.

A more contemporary strong Black woman is Simone Biles, who is the world's most decorated gymnast ever with twenty-five world champion medals, and who in more recent years has been a champion of self-care. At the Tokyo 2020 Olympics, Simone chose to focus on her mental health by withdrawing from the women's team gymnastics final, the all-around, and four individual events. Her brave actions garnered both support and criticism, but the support triumphed. When asked if she would go back to the Tokyo Olympic Games to compete, Simone said, "No. I wouldn't change anything, because everything happens for a reason. And I learned a lot about myself—courage, resilience, how to say no and speak up for yourself."

Another pivotal moment in which Simone exhibited immense poise and courage was when she testified during the Senate Judiciary hearing on Dr. Larry Nassar's sexual abuse investigation. Nassar groomed and sexually abused young girls, including Simone, for decades while being employed as a USA Gymnastics team doctor specializing in overseeing the treatment and physical recovery of young female gymnasts. The system failed her and hundreds of other girls who endured years of abuse at the hands of Nassar. Biles continues to heal and recover with her fellow survivors. Just as importantly, she empowers abuse survivors, alongside her team around the world, by taking such a courageous stand against violence.

All the women in this book blow me away with their guts, courage, smarts, and relentlessness in the face of such oppression. One who has been my hero since I first heard of her is Fannie Lou Hamer, who is well known to those who pay attention to the history of the civil rights movement in America but should be known by everyone for her bravery and persistence.

Fannie was an organizer of the SNCC (the Student Nonviolent Coordinating Committee), a groundbreaking youth-led group of young Black students who led campaigns against racism and segregation. On August 31, 1962, Fannie led volunteers to register rural Black people in Mississippi to vote, which alone speaks to her fortitude. A year later, when she and her associates stopped to get lunch and sat at a "Whites-only" counter in Mississippi, they were asked to leave; they refused the request to leave, the police were called, and they were arrested and roughed up by the Mississippi officers. Fannie herself was beaten bloody in jail and suffered broken bones, a concussion, and permanent injuries such as loss of vision in one of her eyes and kidney damage.

After this violent ordeal, many would have given up trying to fight for the right to vote, but in Fannie's case it seemed to only fire her up more. Despite the extensive trauma she experienced, she grew more dedicated in her fight and remained active in her hugely important work throughout her days.

What is most stunning about awesome Black women is that they invariably must act under an entirely different set of rules while operating in our systemically racist society, and yet they exceed expectations despite their hurdles. They have had to fight to gain freedom and rights, cope with generational trauma, confront micro- and macro-aggressions, protect themselves from all forms of violence, thwart discrimination, and grapple with the intersection of what it means to be Black and a woman.

Black women are set up to fail in institutionally racist societies, but these women thrive beyond anything one can imagine in the face of these inequalities. Every system is built upon and sustained by pushing Black women down, yet they still prevail. So let's give credit to these women and be inspired by them.

What lessons can you take away from these women to apply in your life? We all have difficulties and challenges, albeit rarely of the severity these women had to endure; let them be an inspiration to you.

Finally, when you read these women's stories, reflect on how you have faced challenges in life and dealt with them. Do you offer yourself love and kindness as these women did themselves? Are you resilient in mind, body, and soul like these leaders? Can you use your own stories to help others as these influential figures have done? Black women are a force, and demand to be known for their greatness, and you do too. What better way to celebrate your greatness than with your sisters by your side?

Becca Anderson, author of *The Book of Awesome Women* and *The Book of Awesome Girls*

Chapter 1: SHEroes

Unstoppable Black Women
Who Busted Down Barriers

America inherited the strength, courage, wisdom, love, and dignity of our Black heroines and groundbreakers. We stand on their shoulders—these creators, innovators, and agents of change—and because of their tremendous struggle, we are strong and can conquer whatever challenges this world hands us.

Not content to keep their feet on the ground, Black women have busted through the glass ceiling and flown into outer space (Stephanie Wilson, Mae Jemison). They have challenged the old boys' club and prevailed (Anita Hill). And when the rules in place didn't support them, Black women found a way around the rules to make their mark on history. Aviators like Bessie Coleman and Jill E. Brown broke barriers by taking flight in airplanes even though there were rules in place for many years that kept Black people from earning a commercial pilot's license.

Long relegated to the back seat, Black women have proven they are perfectly capable of getting behind the wheel and driving the vehicle of change beyond the horizon to a new destination. Black women have fought to formalize their participation in professions in which they've worked for centuries informally (Mary Elizabeth Mahoney, nursing). They pushed past the frontier with panache and verve, exploring regions of the planet that had been shut to them for eons (Barbara Hillary, explorer), and they even brought a pet cheetah with them to the stages of Paris (Josephine Baker). If it seemingly can't be done, it's probably a safe bet that a Black woman has done it.

Let us never forget those who broke the unjust rules society used (and sometimes still uses) to limit our progress, those who fought hard to get us to this moment, those who gave light so others could find the way through dark times.

Because of them, all of us can hope to walk in the freedom they fought for, and continue to fight for, on our behalf.

ELIZABETH KEY GRINSTEAD:
Won Her Freedom

Elizabeth Key Grinstead was one of the first Black slaves to sue for freedom in the thirteen colonies. She won her case and freed not only herself but also her son in 1656. Grinstead was the daughter of a Black slave and an Englishman. Her father was taken to court over her paternity and claimed she was the offspring of an unidentified Turkish man. He later accepted responsibility for her and had her baptized in the Church of England, which paved the way for her successful lawsuit. At this time in the colonies, slaves could only be held for a certain period under indentured servant laws that applied to White servants as well. Grinstead's suit claimed that at twenty-five years old, she had served for nineteen years and deserved to be freed. She also successfully argued that her son should be freed since he was born during the period when she should have been free. Grinstead won her case.

JANE MATILDA BOLIN:
Here Comes the Judge

As a mixed-race child, Jane Matilda Bolin was often discriminated against. Several times she was refused service from businesses for being Black. She began to read about the hangings of Black southerners in the NAACP's magazine, *The Crisis*, at an early age, and was influenced by what she read. She became the first Black woman to earn her degree at Yale Law School and the first to join the New York Bar City Association. After becoming the first Black woman in the New York City Law Department, she also became the only (and first) Black female judge in the United

States when she was appointed justice in the Domestic
Relations Court of New York City in 1939. She remained the
only Black female judge in the United States for twenty years.
During her years on the bench, she worked hard to ensure that
childcare services in New York City were fair to Black families.
She also served on the boards of the NAACP and the New York
Urban League.

FRONT AND CENTER

Born in Jamaica, Queens in New York City, **Gwen Ifill** was the
first Black woman to host a nationally televised political talk
show. While at Simmons College in Boston, Gwen interned
with the *Boston Herald-American* newspaper. One day at
work she found a note that read, "N*gg**, go home." She
showed it to her supervisors, who were horrified, but Ifill's
attitude about the matter was that she had work to do, and
this led to her being offered a position at the newspaper
upon her graduation from college. She went on to work for
the *Baltimore Evening Sun,* the *Washington Post,* and after
being told by the *Post* that she wasn't ready to cover Capitol
Hill, she got hired by the *New York Times,* where she covered
the White House. Her first job on television was with NBC,
in 1994, when she was the network's Capitol Hill reporter. In
1999, she made history when she became the moderator for
Washington Week in Review on PBS, the first Black woman to
host a nationally syndicated political program. She was also
the first Black woman to moderate a vice presidential debate,
in 2004, when she moderated the debate between Dick

Cheney and senator John Edwards. Ifill went on to moderate the debate in 2008 between governor Sarah Palin and then senator Joe Biden, who were vying for the vice presidential nomination. Ifill continued hosting the *Washington Week in Review* until her death in 2016.

Tamron Hall is a television broadcast journalist and talk-show host. She worked as a general assignment reporter at local Texas television stations until 1997, when she was hired by WFLD in Chicago, Illinois. There she held several positions as a general assignment reporter, consumer reporter, and as the host of a three-hour morning program called *Fox News in the Morning*. In 2007, she was hired by NBC and MSNBC and landed a one-on-one interview with Barack Obama before he announced his bid for the presidency. Tamron debuted her self-titled, syndicated talk show in 2019. In 2020, the show was honored with three Daytime Emmy nominations, and won the Gracie Award for Outstanding Talk Show.

XERNONA CLAYTON:
First Black On-Air Personality

Xernona Clayton is a civil rights leader and broadcasting executive. When she saw that there were few Black presenters on television, Xernona pointed it out and was hired by WAGA-TV as the host of *Themes and Variations*, which later became the *Xernona Clayton Show*. The program made her the first Black on-air television personality in the South during the years it aired, 1968–75. After Turner Broadcasting was started in 1979, Clayton went to work for them in a career that lasted more than thirty years. When she retired from Turner Broadcasting she was vice president for urban affairs. Clayton continues to live in Atlanta, where she is still active in civil rights and civic affairs.

MAE JEMISON:
First African American Woman in Space (but Not the Last)

How many Americans are multilingual, let alone fluent in Swahili, Japanese, and Russian? Mae Jemison is an engineer and physician as well as a US astronaut—an exceptional achiever by any measure. She was born in 1956 in Decatur, Alabama; her family soon moved to Chicago for a chance at better schools and jobs. As a child, she remembers assuming that she would one day escape terrestrial confines: "I thought by now we'd be going into space like you were going to work." Though her teachers were not especially supportive of her interest in science, her parents encouraged her; she was also attracted to the art of dance and studied ballet, jazz, modern, and African dance. She graduated early and started at Stanford University at age sixteen on a National Achievement Scholarship, graduating in 1977 with a degree in chemical engineering. She also fulfilled the requirements for a BA in African and Afro-American studies. Being a Black female engineering major was no easy thing. As she recalls, "Some professors would just pretend I wasn't there. I would ask a question and a professor would act as if it was just so dumb, the dumbest question he had ever heard. Then, when a White guy would ask the question, the professor would say, 'That's a very astute observation.' "

In 1981, Jemison earned an MD from Cornell Medical College. During her years at Cornell, she spent some of her time providing primary medical care in Cuba, Kenya, and at a Cambodian refugee camp in Thailand. She also kept up her dance studies at the Alvin Ailey School. She interned at Los Angeles County USC Medical Center, and then worked as a general practitioner. She joined the Peace Corps in 1983 and spent the next two years as the medical officer responsible for corps volunteers' health in Sierra Leone and Liberia, as well as assisting with CDC vaccine research.

After completing her hitch with the Peace Corps in 1985, Jemison felt that since fellow Stanford alumna Sally Ride had succeeded in her quest to go to space, the time was ripe to follow her longtime dream, and she applied to join NASA's astronaut training program. The *Challenger* disaster of early 1986 delayed the selection process, but when she reapplied a year later, Jemison made the cut, becoming the first African American woman ever to do so. She was one of only fifteen chosen out of two thousand who tried. When she joined the seven-astronaut crew of the space shuttle *Endeavour* for an eight-day mission in the fall of 1992, she became the first African American woman in space, logging a total of over 190 hours in space. She conducted medical and other experiments while aloft.

After leaving the astronaut corps in spring of 1993, she was named to a teaching fellowship at Dartmouth, and taught there from 1995 to 2002. She is a Professor-at-Large at

Cornell, and continues to advocate for science education and for getting minority students interested in science. She has also founded two companies, the Jemison Group and BioSentient Corp to research, develop, and market various advanced technologies, as well as the Dorothy Jemison Foundation for Excellence, named for her mother, who was a teacher. The Earth We Share science camps are among the foundation's initiatives, as well as the 100 Year Starship project. Jemison has received many awards as well as honorary doctorates from institutions including Princeton, Rensselaer Polytechnic Institute, and DePaul University. Various public schools and a Chicago science and space museum have also been named for her. She has appeared in several TV shows, including an episode of *Star Trek: The Next Generation*, by the invitation of LeVar Burton.

"When I'm asked about the relevance to Black people of what I do, I take that as an affront. It presupposes that Black people have never been involved in exploring the heavens, but this is not so. Ancient African empires—Mali, Songhai, Egypt—had scientists and astronomers. The fact is that space and its resources belong to all of us, not to any one group."

ANITA HILL:
We Always Believed You

Nobody could have guessed that the televised Senate hearings on the nomination of Clarence Thomas to the US Supreme Court would be the top-rated show of 1991. America's collective mouth hung open in amazement at the brouhaha that brewed up around Judge Thomas's worthiness based on the charges of sexual harassment by one Anita Hill. The hearings made the issue of sexual harassment in the workplace into the most hotly debated and analyzed topic of the day, one that still reverberates years later. Prior to Hill's brave stand, sexual harassment was mainly swept under the industrial gray carpeting of most offices, but she singlehandedly forced it to the very center of the national agenda.

The nation and, indeed, the world, watched transfixed as the incredibly poised Hill revealed her experiences of Clarence Thomas as a coworker. With great dignity, she testified that Thomas kept after her to go out with him, referred to himself as "an individual who had a very large penis and...used a name...in pornographic material," and asked her to see "this woman [who] has this kind of breasts that measure this size," in a seemingly endless barrage of ludicrous and lugubrious insults to her as a fellow professional. Senate hearings, usually desert dry and devoid of tabloid titillation, suddenly featured long discussions including the terms "penis" and "pubic hair."

The prelude to the media circus took place when the president announced his choice of "Black Horatio Alger"

Clarence Thomas as the Supreme Court replacement for
the retiring Thurgood Marshall. Anita Hill, a law professor at
the University of Oklahoma, contacted Harriet Grant, the
Judiciary Committee's nominations counsel. She told Grant
that Thomas had harassed her in a sexual and inappropriate
manner when she had worked as his assistant at the Equal
Employment Opportunity Commission (EEOC). She had, in
fact, quit the EEOC because of his behavior and gone into
academia. Grant cc'd the senatorial committee on the
allegations, but the Senate whipped through the approval
process with nary a word about Hill's report and prepared to
vote for confirmation of Thomas. Then journalist SHEro Nina
Totenberg of National Public Radio and *Newsday*'s Timothy
Phelps of New York broke the story wide open to a shocked
public. Seven women from the House of Representatives
marched in protest to the Senate building, demanding of the
sheepish Senate committee to know why they had ignored
Hill's complaint.

Nothing in Hill's background could have prepared her for the
media onslaught. Born in 1956 as the youngest of thirteen
children, she was raised in rural Oklahoma in a deeply
religious family. An outstanding student, she graduated as
valedictorian of her integrated high school, earned top honors
in college, and was one of only eleven Black students out of a
class of 160 at Yale University Law School.

Even though Anita Hill had been promised immunity and
total confidentiality, she appeared before the committee
in a special session, facing the scrutiny of the nation. The
judiciary committee was dismissive, as only old boys can be,
of Hill and her testimony, even going so far as to ask her if

she was taking her revenge as the "woman scorned," and they suggested that she was a patsy for radical liberals and feminists. While her allegations were ultimately disregarded and Clarence Thomas was voted in, Hill's grace under pressure won many admirers who protested the Thomas appointment. The controversy remained headline news for months; polls of public opinion showed Anita Hill gaining and Bush losing points as "I Believe You, Anita!" bumper stickers appeared on thousands of cars across America. For her outspokenness she was awarded the Ida B. Wells Award from the National Coalition of 100 Black Women, and was named one of *Glamour's* Ten Women of the Year in 1991.

Anita Hill's courage of conviction made her a SHEro of the late twentieth century. In her words, "I felt I had to tell the truth. I could not keep silent."

"You just have to tell the truth and that's the most anyone can expect from you, and if you get that opportunity, you will have accomplished something."

JOSEPHINE BAKER:
Black Is Beautiful

Josephine Baker was an American-born French entertainer, French Resistance agent, and civil rights activist who ended up on the FBI watch list after calling out the owner of the Stork

Club for being racist. She left the United States for Paris when she decided she'd had enough of performing for segregated audiences. In Paris, she was known to bring her pet cheetah, Chiquita, with her on stage. Chiquita made things even more exciting for audiences by regularly jumping into the orchestra pit to scare the musicians. Baker was the first Black female lead in a major motion picture, *Zouzou*, in 1934. During World War II, she was part of the French resistance to Nazi occupation and was awarded a medal by the French government for her work as a spy. She was such a fierce advocate for civil rights that, after the death of Dr. Martin Luther King Jr., his widow, Coretta Scott King, offered to let her lead the Civil Rights Movement, but Baker refused out of concern for her children's safety.

JANET COLLINS:
Unapologetically Black

Janet Collins was a ballet dancer, choreographer, and teacher. She was born in New Orleans, Louisiana, in 1917, and moved with her family to Los Angeles when she was four years old. In Los Angeles, Collins received her first dance training at a community center. There were few ballet instructors who would accept Black students at the time. Collins was skilled in dance, and by the age of sixteen she was ready to audition for the prestigious Ballet Russe de Monte-Carlo. She was accepted into the dance troupe, but declined their offer when they required her to whiten her skin and face in order to perform with them. Instead, she joined the Dunham Company and began to dance in New York City. In 1948, she danced in her own choreography at the 92nd Street YMHA. In 1949, she began to dance on Broadway and

received the Donaldson Award for Best Dancer on Broadway
for her work in Cole Porter's *Out of This World*. She was the first
Black ballerina to perform at the Metropolitan Opera, in 1951,
and continued to perform with them until 1955. In later life,
she taught modern dance at Balanchine's School of American
Ballet in New York City and at Marymount Manhattan College
from 1951 until 1972. She retired in 1974 and joined a religious
order. Collins performed despite the harsh racial barriers for
Black ballet dancers. When her company toured the South, an
understudy often had to take over her roles due to rules that
prohibited her from dancing on stage. In 1974, the Alvin Ailey
American Dance Theater paid homage to her as a notable
woman in dance.

MARSHA P. JOHNSON:
Stonewall Liberator

Gender non-conforming Marsha P. Johnson was a gay liberation
and AIDS activist and drag queen. They were born in 1945 in
Elizabeth, New Jersey, one of seven siblings who were raised
in the Mount Teman African Methodist Episcopal Church. In
1966, Johnson left Elizabeth for New York City and transformed
into "Black Marsha," a flamboyant drag queen who often wore
garlands of flowers in her hair. They later changed their stage
name to Marsha P. Johnson, and said the P. stood for "Pay it
no mind." Johnson was present at the Stonewall Uprising and
played a major role in the gay rights movement. They earned
a living through sex work and by performing with drag troupes
such as Angels of Light and Hot Peaches. Johnson was a
founding member of the Gay Liberation Front and cofounded

the Street Transvestite Action Revolutionaries (S.T.A.R.) with their close friend Sylvia Riviera. Later they opened together STAR House, a shelter for homeless LGBT teens in Greenwich Village. Johnson was also a popular part of New York City's art scene and modeled for Andy Warhol. They were an active AIDS activist with ACT UP from 1987–1992. They became known as "the mayor of Christopher Street" due to their welcoming presence in Greenwich Village. Marsha P. Johnson was found dead in the Hudson River in 1992. Police initially ruled the case a suicide, but further investigation led them to reclassify the cause of death as "undetermined."

MARY ELIZA MAHONEY:
Nursing Equality

Mary Eliza Mahoney was the first Black woman in the United States to formally study nursing, earn a degree, and practice nursing as a licensed nurse. At the age of thirty-three Mahoney entered a nursing training program at the New England Hospital for Women and Children. Out of a class of forty, only she and two White classmates graduated from the rigorous sixteen-month program. At the time, it was difficult for Black women to receive training in nursing programs. Schools in the South rejected Black students outright, and schools in the North were not much better at helping Black students matriculate. Mahoney had a prior connection to the hospital, where she had worked as a cook for long sixteen-hour shifts. After receiving her diploma, Mahoney went to work as a private duty nurse, mostly for wealthy White families. She specialized in the care of new mothers and newborns and was praised for her efficiency as a nurse. She was active in fighting for equal rights for Black nurses, who were treated much differently than their White counterparts, and she also served freed Black people and orphans, providing them with their daily needs and shelter. When she retired from nursing, she joined the Nurses Associated Alumnae of the United States and Canada in 1896 but found that they weren't welcoming to Black nurses. In response, she formed her own organization, the National Association of Colored Graduate Nurses, which sought to end discrimination within the nursing profession. In retirement, she was an active supporter of women's rights and supported the suffragist movement. When women were finally allowed the right to vote, she became one of the first women in Massachusetts to register to vote.

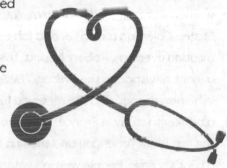

BESSIE COLEMAN:
First in Flight

Born in Texas, Bessie Coleman was the first Black American female pilot. Coleman was the tenth of thirteen children. On her father's side of the family her grandparents were Cherokee, and her mother was Black. Coleman walked four miles to school each day to a one-room segregated schoolhouse where she was an excellent student, especially in mathematics. Every year during the cotton harvest, Coleman had to leave school to work the fields with her family because they were sharecroppers. When she was twelve, Coleman was accepted into the Missionary Baptist Church School on a scholarship. When she graduated high school, she went to the Oklahoma Colored Agricultural and Normal University in Langston, Oklahoma, but she had to drop out when she ran out of savings after just one term.

When she was twenty-three, she moved to Chicago and lived with her brothers while working as a manicurist. She heard stories about pilots returning from World War I and became determined to learn how to fly, but at the time no Blacks or women were allowed to obtain pilot's licenses in the United States. Coleman took a second job to save up money to study aviation overseas. Robert Abbott, the founder and publisher of a Black newspaper, the *Chicago Defender*, publicized her quest in his newspaper, and she received funding from the paper and a banker to study in France. On June 15, 1921, Coleman became the first Black American and the first Native American to earn a pilot's license. People weren't yet traveling much by plane, so in order to make a living as a pilot, Coleman had to learn trick flying and perform stunts at exhibitions and air shows. She was a popular stunt pilot and drew big crowds, and she used her popularity to speak out against racism. She refused to fly in any show where Black people were not allowed to attend.

"The air is the only place free from prejudice."

• • • • •

Jill E. Brown followed in Coleman's footsteps. In the 1970s, Brown was the first Black American woman to fly commercial passenger planes. She flew with Texas International Airlines.

BARBARA HILLARY:
World Explorer

The first known Black American woman to reach both the North and South Poles was Barbara Hillary. At the age of seventy-five, this two-time cancer survivor successfully reached the North Pole, and she reached the South Pole at age seventy-nine. Badass! Hillary was born in 1931 in New York City and raised in Harlem. Her family was impoverished, but she was encouraged to read. She said of her upbringing, "There was no such thing as mental poverty in our home." One of her favorite books was the adventure novel *Robinson Crusoe*. She majored in gerontology at the New School in New York City, and after graduating became a nurse. She worked in that field for fifty-five years before retiring. Sometime in the late '90s, Hillary was diagnosed with lung cancer which required surgery to remove. The surgery resulted in a 25 percent reduction in her breathing ability. This was her second cancer diagnosis: she had been diagnosed with breast cancer in her twenties. She was active in her community, founding the Arverne Action Association, a group dedicated to improving the communities of Arverne and Rockaway. She was founder and editor in chief of *Peninsula Magazine*, a nonprofit multiracial magazine.

After retiring from nursing, Hillary took up adventure. She sledded with dogs in Quebec and photographed polar bears in Manitoba. After learning that no Black woman had ever been to the North Pole, she decided to accept the challenge, even though the expedition would cost $20,000 and require her to learn to ski. She wrote letters to potential sponsors, and eventually raised $25,000 for the trip. On April 23, 2007, at the age of seventy-five, she became one of the oldest people, and the first Black woman, to set foot on the North Pole. Not one to stop at one record, five years later, on January 6, 2011, at the age of seventy-nine, she became the first Black woman to stand on the South Pole. After conquering the poles, Hillary took on climate change. Inspired by her visits to the polar regions, she traveled the world speaking about climate change and calling for reform.

ANNE MOODY:
Freedom Fighter

Anne Moody was born Essa Mae Moody in 1940 in Mississippi. She was the oldest of eight children. Her family was poor, and Moody began working for White families in the area at a young age, cleaning their houses and helping their children with their homework for a few dollars a week. She did this while earning perfect grades at school and helping at church. After she graduated with honors from an all-Black high school, she went to Natchez Junior College, which was also an all-Black school, on a basketball scholarship. She then entered Tougaloo College on an academic scholarship. It was there that she became involved in the civil rights movement, joining

the Congress of Racial Equality, the National Association for
the Advancement of Colored People (NAACP) and the Student
Nonviolent Coordinating Committee. Once she earned her
bachelor's degree, Moody became a full-time civil rights activist
and participated in protests, sit-ins, and marches. At one sit-
in, in a Woolworth's in Jackson, Mississippi, a mob attacked
the protesters and poured mustard, flour, and sugar over their
heads. Another time, Moody and other freedom fighters were
arrested for protesting inside a Jackson post office. In the 1960s,
she moved to New York City and stopped giving interviews.
She used the quiet time to write her memoir *Coming of Age
in Mississippi*, which told about her childhood and the racism
she faced in her young years. In 1964, she went to work for the
Congress of Racial Equality in Canton, Mississippi. She was also
active in the antinuclear movement and wrote two other books,
Mr. Death: Four Stories, a book of fiction, and *Farewell to Too
Sweet*, a sequel to her memoir.

BILLIE HOLIDAY:
Lady Day

Nicknamed "Lady Day," Billie Holiday was an American jazz
and swing singer who revolutionized jazz and swing and had
a lasting impact on musical styles that continues to this day.
Born in 1915 in Philadelphia, Pennsylvania, Holiday had a rough
childhood. Her mother was an unwed teen when she became
pregnant, and her father left soon after she was born. After
being evicted from her parents' house for becoming pregnant,
Holiday's mother arranged for an older half-sister to raise
Holiday in Baltimore.

A frequent truant as a young girl, Holiday was sent to a Catholic reform school, the House of the Good Shepherd, when she was nine years old. While she was in the reform school for nine months, her mother opened a restaurant, and Holiday was paroled to her. She and her mother worked long hours at the restaurant. When she was eleven, her mother discovered a male neighbor trying to rape Holiday, and Holiday was taken into protective custody as a material witness in the rape case against the neighbor. She remained in protective custody at the House of the Good Shepherd until she was twelve. Upon her release, Holiday found work in a brothel and scrubbing floors and marble steps for people in her neighborhood. When her mother moved to Harlem, Holiday followed her a year later. She began singing in nightclubs in Harlem as a young teenager and soon gathered a following.

In 1933, at the age of eighteen, she met producer John Hammond, who arranged for her first recordings with Benny Goodman. She recorded two songs: "Your Mother's Son-In-Law" and "Riffin' the Scotch." The latter became her first hit. From 1935–1941, Holiday's career took off and she recorded a string of hits with pianist/arranger Teddy Wilson. She toured with Count Basie's orchestra in 1937, and in 1938 she made history when Artie Shaw invited her to front his orchestra. It was the first time a Black woman appeared with a White band. In the 1930s, Holiday was introduced to the poem "Strange Fruit." The haunting music that accompanied the poem was written especially for her and it is noted by many music critics to be the first civil rights protest song. When Holiday's recording studio refused to record the song, she went to an independent recording studio, Commodore Records, where she could record whatever she wanted. "Strange Fruit" became an instant hit and sparked a cultural revolution with its vivid depiction of a lynching. In 1939 she wrote "God Bless the Child" with Arthur Herzog. The song has become part of the jazz lexicon and Holiday's recording of it was yet another hit.

In the 1950s, Holiday made over one hundred recordings, including "Lady Sings the Blues." She toured Europe and was a sensation. Her music shaped not only jazz and swing but the blues and rock and roll. She continues to be cited as an influence by many recording artists today. Holiday died in 1959 at the age of forty-four from cirrhosis of the liver.

LENA HORNE:
Legendary Talent

Lena Horne was an American dancer, actress, Grammy-winning singer, and civil rights activist. Her career spanned more than seventy years, and she was a trailblazer in many ways. When she was sixteen, she dropped out of high school and joined the chorus of the Cotton Club in Harlem, and within a year had a featured role in the Cotton Club Parade. She made her Broadway debut in a 1934 production of *Dance with Your Gods*. She sang for a time with Noble Sisso and His Orchestra, and then appeared in the musical revue *Lew Leslie's Blackbirds of 1939*, also on Broadway. She then joined a well-known White swing band, the Charlie Barnet Orchestra. Barnet was one of the first to integrate his band, but Horne still faced discrimination and could not socialize or stay at many of the venues where the band performed. She left the tour rather than suffer the indignation of being treated poorly. She returned to New York where she performed at the Café Society nightclub, which was a venue that was popular with both White and Black crowds.

After a long stint at the Savoy nightclub, Horne's career got a boost when she was featured in *Life* magazine. She became the highest-paid Black entertainer of her time and signed a seven-year contract with MGM. A stipulation of her contract made sure that Horne would not be relegated to playing domestic servants, an industry standard for Black entertainers of the era. Horne was placed in several films, in mostly chorus roles that could easily be edited out for Southern audiences, but she landed two lead roles in *Cabin in the Sky* and *Stormy Weather*. The title song for *Stormy Weather* became a signature favorite of hers that she continued to sing for decades to audiences all around the world. She also starred in the 1969 western *Death of a Gunfighter*.

Her final film role was in 1978 in *The Wiz*, an adaptation of *The Wizard of Oz* that featured an all-Black cast including Diana Ross and Michael Jackson. Horne played Glinda, the good witch. By the end of the 1940s, Horne had filed suit against several clubs for discrimination and joined a leftist group, Progressive Citizens of America. This did not sit well in McCarthy-era America, and Horne soon found herself blacklisted. While she was able to find work at nightclubs and in Europe, she had trouble finding work in film, and went more than a decade without any major roles until the blacklist was ended. Instead, Horne's singing career took off and she made several popular albums including *It's Love* (1955) and *Stormy Weather* (1957).

Her live album *Lena Horne at the Waldorf Astoria* became the best-selling album by a woman at the time for RCA. Horne was very active in the Civil Rights Movement. She performed at rallies around the country representing the NAACP and the National Council for Negro Women. She also participated in the 1963 March on Washington. She retired from performing in 1980 but returned to the stage in 1981 in a one-woman show, *Lena Horne: The Lady and Her Music*. The show ran on Broadway for fourteen months, then toured in the United States and overseas. It won a Drama Desk Award, a special Tony, and two Grammys for its soundtrack.

HARRIET E. ADAMS WILSON:
Provocateur

Like many other literary women, Harriet Wilson was left out of history books. She was the first Black woman to publish a novel in English and the first Black person, male or female, to publish a novel in America.

Sadly, we know precious little about this author. Harriet E. Adams Wilson is believed to have been born in Fredericksburg, Virginia, in 1807 or 1808, and trained in millinery as her trade; she was then deserted and left in poverty by her sailor husband, who impregnated her before the abandonment. Her son from this relationship, George Mason Wilson, died at age seven, a year after the publication of the one novel it is known that Wilson wrote.

Her groundbreaking work, *Our Nig*, a title deliberately chosen for its challenge and daring, was printed by George C. Rand and Avery of Boston. It is believed Wilson self-published *Our Nig* to prove a political point, as evidenced by the full title, *Our Nig, or, Sketches from the Life of a Free Black, in A Two-Story White House, North, Showing That Slavery's Shadows Fall Even There,* with the author credit to "Our Nig."

Our Nig was ignored by reviewers and readers and barely sold. Wilson's work was in the dustbin of lost history until Henry Louis Gates Jr. discovered it and reissued it in 1983. Gates observed that the provocative title probably contributed to the novel's near oblivion. The plot, a marriage between a White woman and a Black man, would have alienated many readers.

TONI MORRISON:
The Truest Eye

Toni Morrison comes from small-town, working-class Ohio, a state that fell "between" on the Civil War issue of slavery, a state with many stops along the underground railroad, and a state where many crosses burned "neither plantation nor ghetto." She has made this her canvas for her rich, original stories that dare to tell uncomfortable truths. And for her daring, she won the Nobel Prize in Literature.

Born in 1931 as Chloe Anthony Wofford, Morrison and her parents worked hard as sharecroppers in their adopted Northern home of Lorain, Ohio. She was keenly interested in language as a child and loved hearing ghost stories, songs, and thundering sermons at church. After high school, she attended Howard University and graduated at the age of twenty-two, following this with a master's from Cornell. Her thesis paper examined the theme of suicide in the works of Virginia Woolf and William Faulkner. She began teaching at Howard and met and married a Jamaican architect, Harold Morrison, with whom she had two sons, Harold Ford and Slade. The marriage was short lived, and Morrison took the children and moved to Syracuse, and then later to New York City, where she was hired by Random House as a senior editor. She worked on several major Black autobiographies of the time, including those of Black Power revolutionary Angela Davis and world champion boxer Muhammad Ali.

As a writer, Toni Morrison made an immediate mark upon America's literary landscape with *The Bluest Eye*, published in 1970, and *Sula*, published three years later. Her next book, *Song of Solomon*, won the National Book Critics Circle Award in 1978. In 1983, she left Random House to devote herself full time to writing, and spent the next five years writing *Beloved*, the fantastical and tragic story of ex-slave Sethe and her children.

Her writing focuses on Black women who had previously been ignored. Her lyrical language combines with both realistic and mythic plot elements to create a distinctive style all her own. In 1993, Morrison won the Nobel Prize in Literature; she was the first Black American to do so. She said, "I am outrageously happy. But what is most wonderful for me personally is to know that the prize has been awarded to an African American. Winning as an American is very special—but winning as a Black American is a knockout."

"Had I loved the life that the state planned for me from the beginning, I would have lived and died in somebody else's kitchen."

MAYA ANGELOU:
How the Caged Bird Sings

Marguerite Johnson's childhood was marked by the hardship of the Depression years in which she grew up. Her parents divorced and packed her off to live with her granny, "Momma" Henderson, who eked out a living in Stamps, Arkansas, running a little general store. Marguerite, known as Maya, attended church devotedly with Momma, who gave her stability and taught her the importance of values and a strong work ethic. The young girl found love and roots with her grandmother and the congregation at their church.

But tragedy struck when she visited her mother in St. Louis for eight months. Her mother had a boyfriend who spent a lot of time at her mother's house and often touched and hugged the seven-year-old overly much, but in her innocence, she mistook it for a father's love. Later, he raped her, and Angelou felt guilty and responsible for his jailing and subsequent death at the hands of other inmates who exacted their own brand of justice on a child molester. She became catatonic because of this onslaught of catastrophic violence. With the support of her family and an adult friend, Bertha Flowers, who introduced her to literature, Angelou gradually re-entered

the world, speaking after five years and graduating first in her eighth-grade class.

Angelou and her mother then moved to San Francisco, where her mother ran a boardinghouse and worked as a professional gambler. Angelou met many colorful characters among the boarders, and threw herself into school, where she flourished. She got pregnant at sixteen and took on the full responsibilities of motherhood with the birth of her son, Guy. For a few years, Angelou walked on the wild side: working at a Creole restaurant, waitressing at a bar in San Diego, even doing an accidental and brief stint as a madam for two lesbian prostitutes. After a two-year marriage to a White man, Angelou started dancing at the Purple Onion and got into showbiz as part of the road show for *Porgy and Bess*, which toured Africa and Europe. After co-organizing Cabaret for Freedom with Godfrey Cambridge for the Southern Christian Leadership Conference (SCLC), Angelou drew Martin Luther King Jr.'s attention for her talent and contribution to the civil rights movement, and he invited her to serve as an SCLC coordinator.

Her career was absolutely astonishing after this point: living in Egypt with Guy and her lover, a South African freedom fighter, and working in Ghana writing for *The African Review*. She remained involved with the theater, writing and performing in plays, acting in *Roots*, and writing several volumes of poetry as well as the script and music for the movie of her autobiography. But it is for the six bestselling volumes of her autobiography, starting with *I Know Why the Caged Bird Sings*, that she will go down in literary history. (*The New York Times* called her "one of the geniuses of Afro-American serial autobiography.") Written with captivating honesty, color, and verve, they are read by youth and adults alike for their inspirational message. Listen to this powerful passage from *I Know Why the Caged Bird Sings*: "If growing up is painful for the Southern Black girl, being aware of her displacement is the rust on the razor that threatens the throat. It is an unnecessary insult." When she was criticized for not being completely factual as a writer, Maya responded, "There's a world of difference between truth and facts. Facts can obscure truth."

Maya Angelou, whose name was combined from a nickname her brother gave her and a variation on her first husband's name, truly reinvented herself. No moment in her wonderfully colorful life illustrates this as much as her reading of her beautiful poem "On the Pulse of Morning" at President Bill Clinton's first inauguration. She had come a long way, from the scared and silent little seven-year-old to a woman come fully into her power, unafraid to share that with the world.

"The ability to control one's own destiny...comes from constant hard work and courage."

JACKIE ORMES:
First Professional Cartoonist

For many years, reading and writing were not expected of Black people—for many enslaved Black people it was against the law to learn to read and write. As a result, there weren't many Black-centered books with Black characters, and rarely any children's books with Black characters. When Black characters did appear in mainstream publications, they were usually stereotypical images of Sambo-like characters with big lips and other exaggerated features that reinforced stereotypes about Black people.

Black cartoonists have had to deal with a lot of racism within the cartoon industry. During the golden age of comics, which lasted from the 1930s through the 1950s, few Black cartoonists were recognized for their talent, because they were only being published in Black press outlets like the *Chicago Defender.* In 1947, All-Negro Comics became the first comic book company with an all-Black staff. The first issue of the magazine they created was a stunning success, but they never printed a second edition because White paper mill owners refused to sell them paper to print the issue.

It wasn't until 1970 that the Coretta Scott King Awards were created to reward Black illustrators and writers for creating children's books for Black readers. As the demand for Black illustrators to fill the pages of books grew, so did the opportunities. Now there are many Black illustrators who create illustrations for books and cartoons.

Jackie Ormes is widely considered to be the first professional Black cartoonist in America. She created four comic strips: *Torchy Brown in Dixie to Harlem* (1937), *Candy* (1945), *Patty Jo 'n' Ginger* (1946), and *Torchy Brown, Heartbeats* (1950). After high school, Ormes took her first job as a proofreader for the *Pittsburgh Courier.* She began contributing to the news stories at the paper and eventually began to draw comics for them. In 1945, she went to work for the *Chicago Defender* as a comic artist and contributing journalist. In 1946, she created the comic *Patty Jo 'n' Ginger*. The comic was so popular that a doll was created from the character Patty Jo, the first Black doll created from a comic strip.

THE COURAGEOUS NANCE LEGINS-COSTLEY

Nance Legins-Costley was the first slave freed by Abraham Lincoln, in 1841, twenty years before the civil war, in a court case that went to the Illinois Supreme Court. She was born in 1813 in Kaskaskia, Illinois, into the household of Colonel Thomas Cox, who owned her parents despite Illinois being a free territory at that time. In 1827, she was sold to a man named Nathan Cromwell for $151, but she resisted being taken from the only household she had ever known and was locked in a windowless room for a week as punishment. She was then forced to go to her new home. Meanwhile, Colonel Cox tried to have the sale of his slaves reversed and took the case to court. Legins-Costley showed courage when she testified that she had not gone willingly to the new home and was not living there by her own choice. But the court decided she had no say in whether she was sold or not. The case went to appeal several times and each time she was declared a piece of property with no say over whether she could be bought and sold. During the years that her case was in the court system, Nance married a free Black man named Benjamin Costley. When she was sold again to an abolitionist named David Bailey, a relative of Nathan Cromwell's went to court to try

to take over possession of her. David Bailey hired Abraham
Lincoln to argue Legins-Costley's case before the Illinois
Supreme Court, and he won the case, arguing that since every
person in the state of Illinois was free regardless of color, no
one could be bought or sold. Legins-Costley was freed! Not
only was she freed, the three children she had given birth to
in the years her case was in the court system were declared
free as well. She lived the rest of her life in a log cabin in Pekin,
Illinois, with her husband and children.

ELLA BAKER:
For the Sake of the Next Generation

Ella Baker was born in 1903 in Norfolk, Virginia. She developed a
sense of social justice early from listening to her grandmother's
stories about her time as a slave. Baker's grandmother had been
beaten for refusing to marry a man the slave owner wanted her
to marry. Her grandparents bought a piece of the plantation
on which they had been enslaved once they were freed and
farmed the land. They were very proud of this and became
successful farmers. Baker studied at Shaw University, where she
graduated as the class valedictorian in 1927. During her time at
Shaw, she spoke out against school policies she thought were
unfair. After graduating, she moved to New York City where she
began joining civil rights organizations like the Young Negroes
Cooperative League, the purpose of which was to improve the
economic situation for Black people. In 1940, she joined the
NAACP as a field secretary and served as the director of several
branches between 1943 and 1946. In 1955, Baker cofounded

In Friendship, an organization that raised money to fight
Jim Crow Laws. In 1957, she helped Dr. Martin Luther King Jr.
organize the Southern Christian Leadership Conference. When
students in Greensboro, North Carolina, were refused service at
a Woolworth's lunch counter, Baker called a meeting at Shaw
University for student activists that led to the formation of the
Student Nonviolent Coordinating Committee, an organization
that was dedicated to nonviolent resistance. They helped the
Congress of Racial Equality organize the Freedom Rides in 1961.
Baker was given a nickname, "Fundi," a Swahili word that means
a person who teaches the next generation. Until her death in
1986, Baker continued to be a champion of civil rights.

• • • • •

Whether they conquered the arctic or championed for civil
rights or appeared on the cover of *Vogue*, these women knew
how to take life by storm. Unwilling to accept the status quo,
they became the best of their generation and changed life for
all of us.

Chapter 2: Hidden Figures No Longer

Brilliant Inventors and Scientists

The contributions Black women have made in the fields of science and invention are stunning and have shaped the world for the better. Thanks to **Mary Beatrice Davidson Kenner**, the inventor of sanitary pads, for example, women can keep their skirts, pants, and sheets from getting dirty during their period. Racial discrimination prevented Kenner from filing her patent for the sanitary napkin for more than thirty years; she also never made a penny off its invention. Yet she went on to invent a toilet tissue holder and a carrier attachment for an invalid walker.

When she was challenged by life in a high-crime neighborhood with a slow police response time, working different shifts from her husband, **Marie Van Brittan Brown** invented the world's first home security system (and closed-circuit television system too!), and her product became the prototype for most modern home security systems.

Neither Kenner nor Brown took problems lying down, and their attitude is typical of many of the Black pioneers in the fields of invention and science. In 1884, **Judy W. Reed** was the first Black woman to file and receive a US patent. Her invention is called a "Dough Kneader and Roller," and it was an improvement on existing dough rollers of the day; it allowed the dough to mix more evenly. Because women often signed the patent applications using their first and/or middle initials to disguise their gender, and because the patent application does not include race, it is unknown if there were any earlier Black female inventors.

Black women persevere. **Dr. Jane Cooke Wright** not only developed chemotherapy treatments, but she was also one of the first scientists to test on human tissue instead of mice. She also pioneered the use of the drug methotrexate for breast and skin cancers. The inventor of laser cataract surgery techniques, **Dr. Patricia E. Bath** was the first Black woman doctor to receive a patent for a medical purpose; her "Laserphaco Probe" for cataract treatment enabled surgeons to restore sight to many people who were blind for as long as thirty years. In 1933, **Ruth Ella Moore** became the first Black American woman to earn a PhD in natural science; she studied bacteriology and taught at Howard University, where she was chairwoman of the department of microbiology. Biomedical scientist and environmental lawyer **Adrienne Hollis** used her time at Florida Agricultural and Mechanical University to help create a toxicology curriculum for communities where environmental racism would likely happen. The first African Canadian public health nurse, **Bernice Redmon** had to leave Canada and travel to the United States to receive an education, because Black people were barred from attending nursing school in Canada in the 1940s. She studied in Virginia instead, and then returned home to practice nursing.

Not knowing about these women is understandable. Historically, Black women haven't received the same accolades as their White peers. But if there is a problem in the world, leave it to a Black woman to find a solution. As a high school senior, **Dr. Venita Simpson** applied for a scholarship, but despite her 4.0 GPA, her guidance counselor recommended another student of privilege for the scholarship. Simpson still became the first Black woman to complete a neurosurgery residency at Baylor College of Medicine since the program began in 1956. She's also a lieutenant commander in the US Navy.

Despite the roadblocks put in place to keep them out of secondary education programs and away from the patent office, Black women have been innovating for centuries. Becoming a Black scientist or inventor was next to impossible for many years because of laws that kept Black people and White people separate and because enslaved Black people were not allowed to read or write. Yet these women didn't let anything stop them on their quests to becoming trailblazers in invention or science. Their stories are here to show you that nothing can stop you if you work hard and have faith in yourself, and to teach you all about the marvelous world of Black science and invention.

FLEMMIE PANSY KITTRELL:
Nourishing the World

Dr. Flemmie Pansy Kittrell was the first Black woman to earn a PhD in nutrition.

Kittrell graduated high school with honors and her family encouraged her to go to Hampton Institute for a degree in home economics. Her professors were so impressed with her work at Hampton that they encouraged her to go to graduate school. Very few Black women—very few women of any race—attended graduate school at the time, but Kittrell won a scholarship to Cornell University, a prestigious Ivy League college, and in 1936 she became the first Black woman to receive her PhD from the school. In the early years of her career she taught high school, but she soon accepted a position at Bennett College in Greensboro, North Carolina. She later returned to Hampton Institute as a professor of nutrition, and quickly became the dean of the school of home economics.

In 1947, Kittrell began an international crusade to help children suffering from hunger. She believed that lack of access to food was a huge problem for poor people, and so she combined her home economic classes with courses in science and engineering to try to solve it. She traveled to Liberia in Africa where she discovered that, while Liberian people typically had full bellies, they weren't receiving enough nutrients on their diets of cassava and rice. She introduced different ways to add more protein into their diets, such as through fishing. Kittrell traveled the world in pursuit of her studies. Along with Liberia, she traveled to India, Japan, West Africa, Central Africa, Guinea, and Russia. She helped set up a training program for home economics in Baroda College in India, and back at Howard, Kittrell used her position to recruit students from all over the world. In the 1960s, she helped establish the Head Start program for pre-kindergarten children. She was awarded the Scroll of Honor from the National Council of Negro Women in 1961.

REBECCA LEE CRUMPLER:
Our First Physician

Prior to 1860, it was rare for Black men or women to be accepted into medical schools, but the heavy fighting during the Civil War meant that doctors were needed, and Rebecca Lee Crumpler was the first Black woman in the United States to earn a medical degree and practice medicine. Crumpler had a hard time at her job, providing medical care for freed slaves who were turned away by White doctors. People made fun of her and said the "MD" after her name stood for "Mule Driver," and many pharmacists refused to fill her prescriptions because she was Black. She persevered. In fact, Crumpler is believed to be the first Black American and the first American woman to write a medical book. Her *Book of Medical Discourses* was published in 1883; in it, she talks about illnesses in young children and women.

"I early conceived a liking for, and sought every opportunity to relieve the suffering of others."

ROGER ARLINER YOUNG:
First Zoologist

In 1940, Roger Arliner Young became the first Black American woman to earn a PhD in zoology. Born in 1899 in Clifton Forge, Virginia, Young moved to Pennsylvania when she was a child. Her family was very poor. Young's mother was disabled and many of the family's resources went for her care. She attended Howard University with the intent of studying music but was called to science after a couple of years of study. In 1924, her first article, "On the excretory apparatus in *Paramecium*," was published in the journal *Science*, making her the first Black American woman to research and professionally publish in this field.

DOROTHY LAVINIA BROWN:
First Southern Surgeon

The mother of Dorothy Lavinia Brown surrendered her to an orphanage at the age of five months, and Brown was raised in the orphanage until she was twelve years old. When attending Bennett College and Meharry College, she supported herself by working as a domestic servant. In 1949, she became a resident at Hubbard Hospital of Meharry despite opposition to having women train as surgeons. After completing her residency, Brown became the first Black female surgeon to operate in the South. In 1956, she became the first single woman in the state of Tennessee to adopt a child. In 1966, she became the first Black woman elected to the Tennessee State Assembly, a position she held for two years. While in the legislature, Brown advocated for abortion, equal rights, and women's rights. Brown also became an accomplished surgeon and was popular on the speaking circuit. She was the first Black female to be elected Fellow of the American College of Surgeons.

HELEN OCTAVIA DICKENS:
First Black Female Ob-Gyn in Philadelphia

Helen Octavia Dickens became the first Black American female to be admitted to the American College of Surgeons. Her father was a former slave and a water boy during the Civil War; her mother was a domestic servant. Because the family struggled financially, both her parents instilled in her the importance of getting an education. Dickens attended a desegregated high school. At Crane Junior College, Dickens took pre-medical classes, but faced a lot of discrimination and prejudice from her White classmates. To avoid hearing their comments and seeing their gestures, Dickens sat at the front of the class so she could focus on the professor. At the University of Pennsylvania, where she earned her master's degree in medical science, Brown was one of only two female students and the only Black student. She completed an internship at Chicago's Provident Hospital, where she worked with the poor and treated tuberculosis. After working at Provident for seven years, Dickens decided she wanted to study obstetrics and gynecology and attended the Perelman

School of Medicine at the University of Pennsylvania. Dickens specialized in obstetrics and gynecology and was challenged by her patients' living conditions. During one delivery, Dickens discovered there was no electricity, so she had to move the bed and deliver the baby by streetlight. To help her patients who were in dire financial need, Dickens established four beds at the Aspiranto Health Home, a three-story healthcare clinic in North Philadelphia. After passing her board examinations, Dickens became the first Black female Ob-Gyn-certified doctor in Philadelphia.

JANE COOKE WRIGHT:
Highest-Ranking Black
Female Physician

Jane Cooke Wright was the first Black American woman to become president of the New York Cancer Society. Wright's father was one of the first Black graduates from Harvard Medical School and instilled in her an appreciation for education at a very young age. She graduated with honors from New York Medical College in 1945 and went to work at Bellevue Hospital as an intern from 1945–1946. She completed her residency at New York's Harlem Hospital. After her residency, she continued at Harlem Hospital as a visiting physician, and took a job as doctor for New York City's public schools. After six months with the school district, Wright left to join her father, who was director of the Cancer Research Foundation at Harlem Hospital. At the time, chemotherapy was still in its investigative stages. Wright's father had directed the foundation to study anti-cancer chemicals, and together they researched different combinations of chemicals that could fight cancer. There were several human trials in which Wright administered chemotherapy to patients. Some successfully entered remission.

After her father's death in 1952, Wright was named director of the Cancer Research Foundation. She was just thirty-three years old. In 1955, Dr. Wright became an associate professor of surgical research at New York University and director of cancer chemotherapy research at New York University Medical Center. In 1964, President Lyndon B. Johnson appointed Dr. Wright to the President's Commission on Heart Disease, Cancer, and Stroke. In 1967, she was named professor of surgery, head of the Cancer Chemotherapy Department, and associate dean at New York Medical College, her alma mater. At a time when Black women physicians numbered only a few hundred in the entire United States, Dr. Wright was the highest-ranking Black woman at a nationally recognized medical institution.

In 1971, Dr. Jane Wright became the first female president of the New York Cancer Society. During her forty-year career, Dr. Wright published many research papers on cancer and chemotherapy, and led cancer researchers on trips to Africa, China, Eastern Europe, and the Soviet Union.

ALEXA CANADY:
First Black Female Neurosurgeon

Alexa Canady became the first Black American female to practice neurosurgery. She was born in Lansing, Michigan, in 1951. The only two Black children in their school, she and her younger brother faced a lot of discrimination. One time, a teacher even switched her test grades with those of a White student to hide how smart young Canady really was. But her parents taught her the importance of education, and she worked hard to overcome hardships. She graduated with honors from her high school and went to the University of Michigan. At first, Canady majored in mathematics, but she did not love her math classes and almost dropped out of college. She then discovered that she loved zoology, the study of animals. After she got her bachelor's degree, Canady learned that not many Black people were studying medicine, so she decided to go to the University of Michigan Medical School. While she was there, she discovered her passion for helping people with medical problems. She specialized in pediatric neurosurgery, which meant she performed operations on children who had brain diseases or injuries. Her advisers discouraged her from a career in pediatric neurosurgery and she had trouble finding an internship, but she didn't give up. Finally, she was accepted as an intern at Yale New Haven Hospital in 1975, where she was the first woman to join the program.

Canady worked for many years as a pediatric neurosurgeon at Detroit's Henry Ford Hospital. She retired and moved to Florida in 2001, but she didn't stay retired for very long. After discovering there were no pediatric neurosurgeons working in her area, she went back to work part time at Pensacola's Sacred Heart Hospital. Canady has been quoted as saying, "The greatest challenge I faced in becoming a neurosurgeon was believing it was possible." Alexa retired for a second time in 2012. She continues to encourage young women to go into medicine and neurosurgery.

JOYCELYN ELDERS:
"I Am Who I Am Because I'm a Black Woman."

Joycelyn Elders, appointed by President Bill Clinton, became the first Black female to serve as US surgeon general. She was born in 1933 in Schaal, Arkansas, to a poor family of sharecroppers. She worked as a nurse's aide and physical therapist before attending the University of Arkansas Medical School. After medical school, she specialized in pediatrics. In 1987, then-governor Bill Clinton appointed Elders to head up the Arkansas Department of Health. While in this position, Elders helped lower the teen pregnancy rate in the state through education and by making birth control more widely available. She also increased the child immunization rate, helped expand HIV testing, increased breast cancer screenings, and improved elderly care. In 1992, she was elected president of the Association of State and Territorial Health Officers.

In January 1993, President Bill Clinton appointed her to the surgeon general's position, making her the first Black woman to hold the post. His selection of her was not without controversy, which Elders felt was racist in nature. She said of her critics,

---

"Some people in the American Medical Association, a certain group of them, didn't even know that I was a physician. They were passing a resolution to say that from now on every surgeon general must be a physician—which was a knock at me...They don't expect a black female to have accomplished what I have and to have done the things that I have."

Elders drew criticism for suggesting that drugs should be legalized, that "we really need to get over this love affair with the fetus and start worrying about children," and for suggesting that educating children about masturbation as a normal part of a healthy sex life should be considered to help lower the number of AIDS cases. This last comment drew the ire of the White House, and President Clinton forced Elders to resign in December 1994. After leaving the White

House, Elders returned to the University of Arkansas for
Medical Sciences as a professor of pediatrics. Dr. Elders is a
popular speaker and is active on the lecture circuit, where she
discusses teen pregnancy and sex education.

FAYE WATTLETON:
Footsteps to Follow

Faye Wattleton was working as a student nurse at Harlem
Hospital when one case drew her attention to the importance
of safe and legal abortion. It was "a really beautiful
seventeen-year-old girl," she recalls. "She and her mother had
decided to induce an abortion by inserting a Lysol douche
into her uterus. It killed her." That's when Wattleton became
a reproductive-rights activist, holding various positions in
public health administration and the Planned Parenthood
Federation of America (PPFA) before being elected in 1978
to the PPFA presidency. Ironically, Wattleton was giving birth
when she won!

She carries the triple honor of being the first woman, the first
African American, and the youngest person ever to head up
the PPFA. Over the years, she has worked valiantly to fight
the barriers constantly being put in the way of reproductive
rights—President Reagan's "squeal rule" to notify parents of
the distribution of birth control or information, the "gag rule"
preventing abortion counseling, and the Supreme Court's
challenge to Roe v. Wade. She resigned the presidency in
1992. Pointing to her contributions, Arthur J. Kopp of People

for the American Way noted "her remarkable ability to communicate difficult issues [has] made her a giant in the ongoing battle to preserve Americans' fundamental liberties."

HENRIETTA LACKS:
Immortal

Henrietta Lacks was a housewife and tobacco farmer whose cancer cells are the source of the first immortalized cancer cell line, and whose cells continue to be used for research. Lacks was born in Roanoke, Virginia, in 1920. When she was four years old, her mother died giving birth to her tenth child, and the family was split up. Lacks was sent to live with her maternal grandfather in Clover, Virginia, where she began farming tobacco at a young age to help support her family. She was married in 1951 and had five children. Shortly after she was married, her family moved to Turner Station, Maryland, for better job opportunities.

After giving birth to her last child, Lacks was diagnosed with cervical cancer. Some of her cells were sent to a researcher, George Gey, at Johns Hopkins, without her permission. Dr. Gey discovered that Lacks's cells were unlike any of the other cells he studied. The other cells would all die off quickly, but Lacks's cells doubled every twenty-to-twenty-four hours. Lacks's incredible immortal cells, named the HeLa line, have been used in medical research for many different things. They allow doctors to perform experiments without testing on humans, and have been used to test the effects of toxins, drugs, hormones, and virus cells on cancer cells. They were also instrumental in the development of the polio vaccine and studies of the human genome. Although Henrietta Lacks died of cervical cancer in 1951, at the age of thirty-one, her life has saved many others.

• • • • •

Black women have also been instrumental in other areas of science aside from the medical field. Black women work in many different fields of science. Many of them have been unrecognized for their contributions, though history is catching up with these pioneers as we learn more about unsung heroes. They have been involved with NASA since the very early days of the space program. President John F. Kennedy's quest to put a man on the moon was largely completed by women who provided the behind-the-scenes technical support the agency needed to fulfill its goal. **Katherine Johnson**, **Dorothy Vaughan**, and **Mary Jackson** helped launch the space program at NASA and are veterans of the "human computer" segregation of women of color at the organization. Their story inspired Margot Lee Shetterly's book *Hidden Figures: The American Dream and the Untold Story of the Black Female Mathematicians Who Helped Win the Space Race*, which was recently adapted into an acclaimed motion picture that stars Taraji P. Henson, Janelle Mona´e, and Octavia Spencer, among others.

KATHERINE JOHNSON:
A "Human Computer"

Katherine Johnson was a mathematician whose calculations helped the first US-piloted space flights and many others that followed. She was born in 1918 in White Sulphur Springs, West Virginia, and was interested in math from a very young age. Because schools in her hometown did not offer public education to Black students past the eighth grade, Johnson had to travel to attend high school in Institute, West Virginia, on the campus of West Virginia State College. She was so advanced that she began attending high school at the age of ten and graduated at just fourteen years old. She then began college at West Virginia State and very quickly took every math class the college offered. The school added math classes just to accommodate her love of the subject. She graduated with a degree in mathematics and French at the age of eighteen.

Johnson wanted to become a research mathematician, but it was difficult to find a career in that field for Black people, especially women. After one of her family members told her that the National Advisory Committee for Aeronautics (NACA) was looking for mathematicians, Johnson applied and was hired. Johnson worked as a human computer, figuring out things like gust alleviation for aircrafts. Her office was segregated, which meant that she had to eat lunch in a different room than her White coworkers and use a separate bathroom, even though she was smarter than many of them. When she first worked for NACA, no women were allowed to put their names on any of the scientific papers they wrote, so her male coworkers often took credit for work she had done.

From 1958 until she retired, Johnson worked as an aerospace technologist. As part of her job, she calculated the trajectory for the flight of astronaut Alan Shepard, the first American in space. She also calculated the launch window for the 1961 Mercury mission and created navigation charts for astronauts. President Barack Obama presented her with the Presidential Medal of Freedom in 2015. She spent her later years encouraging students to go into science, technology, engineering, or mathematics.

"I like to learn. That's an art and a science."

DOROTHY VAUGHAN:
Space Calculator

Dorothy Vaughn was a mathematician and human computer who worked for NACA and later NASA. She was born in 1910 in Kansas City, Missouri. When she was seven years old, her family moved to Morgantown, West Virginia. Vaughn was valedictorian of her high school class and attended Wilberforce University on a full-tuition scholarship. She majored in mathematics while at college. After graduating, she was urged to attend graduate school, but instead went to work as a high school teacher to help her family out during the Great Depression. After marrying in 1932, she and her family moved to Newport News, Virginia, where she taught high school. Virginia's public schools were segregated during her entire teaching career, which encompassed fourteen years.

In 1943, Vaughn began a twenty-eight-year career as a mathematician and programmer with NACA at the Langley Research Center. She specialized in calculations for flight paths, the Scout Project, and computer programming. At Langley, Vaughn was assigned to West Area Computers, a segregated unit of Black human computers. Because of Jim Crow laws, the workforce at Langley was segregated, and the Black women used separate bathroom and dining areas from their White counterparts. In 1949, Vaughn was made supervisor at West Area Computers when a White supervisor died unexpectedly. The first Black female to hold a supervisory role at Langley, she held the interim role for years before being formally promoted to the supervisory position. While at NACA, Vaughn became involved with the space program under President Kennedy, and stayed on when NACA transitioned into NASA. One of her calculations was involved in John Glenn's launch into orbit. In addition to her full-time career, Vaughn raised six children on her own after her husband's death in 1955. She was awarded the Congressional Medal of Honor posthumously in 2019.

MARY JACKSON:
A Pioneer both in Research and Ending Discrimination at NASA

Mary Jackson, born in 1921, was an African American mathematician who rose to the position of NASA's first Black female engineer. She had earned double-major bachelor's degrees in mathematics and physical science in 1942, but worked as a schoolteacher, bookkeeper, and clerk for nearly the next decade before being recruited in 1951 to the gender- and color-segregated human computer department at NACA, NASA's predecessor as an aerospace agency. A couple of years later, she took another NASA position as an engineer, working on the supersonic pressure tunnel; she was encouraged to do graduate-level physics and math studies so she could be promoted to an engineering position. These University of Virginia night courses were given at an all-White high school; she had to petition the city of Hampton, Virginia, her hometown, for special permission to attend classes with White students. Nevertheless, she persisted, and in 1958 became an aerospace engineer at what was now renamed NASA, researching airflow around aircraft.

While her contributions to aerodynamic studies were significant, after many years Jackson took an in-depth look at the inequalities built into the agency and saw that she could have the greatest impact in a formal human resources role. In 1979, she took on a new role as an affirmative-action program manager and federal women's program manager at NASA, taking a cut in pay to do so. In that position, she was able to make changes that empowered women and people of color and helped managers to see the capabilities of their Black and female employees. Even when NASA administrators were finally forced to acknowledge Black women's work at the agency, the public generally had no idea about the contributions of the Black women of NASA.

KATHRYN PEDDREW:
Chemist and Calculator

Kathryn Peddrew was an African American woman who made mathematical and research contributions to the early development of US space flight, despite racial and gender discrimination. Born in 1922, she graduated from college with a chemistry degree and had hoped to join a research team led by one of her college professors studying quinine-caused deafness in New Guinea, but was denied the opportunity because the team had made no arrangements to house women separately from men. (At the time, coed housing would have been considered a scandal.) Instead, Peddrew decided to apply for a position in the aeronautical agency's chemistry research division. She was hired by NACA, which would later become NASA, in 1943. But when administrators learned she was Black, they changed their minds about placing her in the chemistry job and transferred her to the computing division instead, which had a segregated section for the Black female human computers— even though she had a degree in chemistry. Over the course of her career at NACA/NASA, Peddrew worked in both aeronautics and aerospace, and studied balance in the Instrument Research Division. She spent her entire career there, retiring in 1986.

CHRISTINE DARDEN:
When You Hear a Sonic Boom, Think of Her

Racial and gender discrimination in hiring practices at NASA hadn't improved much by the time Christine Darden applied for a position in the late 1960s. Darden, despite her master's degree in applied mathematics, which qualified her for a position as an engineer, was instead assigned to the segregated female human computer pool, as were several other Black female scientists. She approached her supervisor, asking why men with the same education as her had wider opportunities, and gained a transfer to an engineering job in 1973, becoming one of a tiny number of female aerospace engineers at NASA's Langley Research Center. In this role, she worked on the science of sonic-boom minimization, writing computer test programs as well as more than fifty research articles in the field of high-lift wing design. In 1983, Darden earned a doctorate, and by 1989 she was appointed to the first of a number of management and leadership roles at NASA, including that of technical leader of the sonic-boom team within the High-Speed Research Program, and was named director of the Program Management Office of the Aerospace Performing Center in 1999. She worked at NASA until her retirement in 2007.

"I was able to stand on the shoulders of those women who came before me, and women who came after me were able to stand on mine."

ANNIE EASLEY:
Girls Who Code

Annie Easley was an African American computer scientist and mathematician as well as an actual rocket scientist. After joining NASA in 1955, she became a leading member of the team that wrote the computer code used for the Centaur rocket stage. Easley's program was the basis for future programs that have been used in military, weather, and communications satellites. After taking college courses, first one and then two or three at a time, she had to take three months of unpaid leave in 1977 to finish her degree; NASA normally paid for work-related education, but every time she applied for aid she was turned down. However, once she finished her bachelor's degree, personnel decided she had to undergo yet more specialized training to be considered a "professional." Despite this discrimination, Easley continued as a NASA research scientist until 1989, making contributions in many areas, including hazards to the ozone layer, solar energy and wind power, and electric vehicles. She also worked concurrently as NASA's equal-employment opportunity officer, a position where she could address discrimination problems in the agency and work for fairer and more diverse employee recruitment.

SHIRLEY ANN JACKSON:
Black Brainiac

Shirley Jackson is a highly regarded physicist and the first Black woman to earn a PhD from MIT. Her doctoral research project was in theoretical particles. Jackson has gone on to receive numerous awards and the highest praise not only for her work in elementary particles but also for her advocacy of women and minorities in the science field. In 1995, Vice President Al Gore celebrated her contributions and her drive to be the best at her swearing-in as chairman of America's Nuclear Regulatory Commission. Gore told the audience that a four-year-old Shirley Ann Jackson informed her mother that one day she was going to be called "Shirley the Great." Jackson made good on her promise as she pushed down barriers of segregation and bigotry to become one of the top scientists in the nation.

"I had to work alone...at some level you have to decide you will persist in what you're doing and that you won't let people beat you down."

VALERIE THOMAS:
Illusion Generator

Valerie Thomas is an American scientist and inventor. As a young girl in Maryland, she became intrigued by technology while watching her father work on their television set. When her dad didn't encourage her interest, she began her electronics education herself at her local library. There, she found and checked out *The Boys' First Book on Electronics.*

Thomas went to an all-girls school where studying science and mathematics was not championed, but she didn't give up on her dream. In fact, when she went to college at Morgan State University, she majored in physics and then went on to work at the National Aeronautics and Space Administration, or NASA, as a data analyst. She became fascinated with an illusion generator she saw at a scientific exhibition, and invented her own, using mirrors to project a three-dimensional illusion. It is a technology that NASA still uses today.

At NASA, Thomas worked to develop their satellite imaging program for Landsat, a satellite that takes images of Earth's resources from outer space. Thomas continued to work for NASA until her retirement in 1995. While there, she conducted research related to Halley's Comet, the ozone layer, and supernovas. She received several awards from NASA, including the Goddard Space Flight Center Award of Merit and the NASA Equal Opportunity Medal. She continues to mentor young students through various programs today.

EUPHEMIA LOFTON HAYNES:
Doctor of Mathematics

Euphemia Lofton Haynes was the first Black American woman to earn a PhD in mathematics. After her graduation, she went

on to have a storied career in public education in Washington,
DC. She taught for forty-seven years and was the first female
to chair the DC Board of Education. While in her role with the
board, Haynes lobbied for an end to the track system, which
left many Black students unprepared for the possibility of
college. She was also a professor of mathematics at the
University of the District of Columbia, and chaired the Division
of Mathematics and Education, which she helped create with a
mind toward training Black teachers. Haynes retired from
teaching in 1959 but went on to establish the Department of
Mathematics at the University of the District of Columbia. She
was an active member of her community, serving as the first
vice president of the Archdiocesan Council of Catholic Women,
was chair of the Advisory Board of Fides
Neighborhood House, served on the
Committee of International Social
Welfare and the Executive Committee of
the National Social Welfare Assembly,
was secretary and member of the
Executive Committee of the DC
Health and Welfare Council, served
on the local and national
committees of the United Service
Organization, and was a member of the National
Conference of Christians and Jews, the Catholic Interracial
Council of Washington, the National Urban League, the
NAACP, the League of Women Voters, and the American
Association of University Women.

YVONNE CLARK:
An American Engineer

Yvonne Clark was an American engineer. She was the first woman to earn a bachelor's degree in mechanical engineering at Howard University, and the first Black woman to earn a master's in engineering management at Vanderbilt University. Raised in Louisville, Kentucky, she liked to see how mechanical things worked. From a very early age, she enjoyed building things and fixing them. She was not allowed to take a mechanical drawing class in school because she was a girl, but in high school she took an aeronautics course. She joined the school's Civil Air Patrol program, where she learned how to shoot a gun and took flight lessons in a simulator. Clark graduated from high school at sixteen and spent the next two years studying at Boston Latin School. She then went on to study engineering at Howard University, where she was the only woman in her class. She was not allowed to march at graduation with her male classmates. Instead, she received her diploma in the university president's office.

Clark had a difficult time finding a job after she graduated from Howard, because of her gender and because she was Black. She finally found a job with Frankford Arsenal Gauge Labs in Philadelphia, and later with the Radio Corporation of America (RCA) in Montclair, New Jersey. After marrying, Clark moved to Nashville, Tennessee, and was hired as an engineering professor at Tennessee State University, where she was the only woman professor in the engineering department. During summer breaks, she worked a variety of engineering jobs, including weapons research at Frankford Arsenal and

designing containers to bring back lunar samples for NASA.
She earned her master's degree at Vanderbilt University in
1972, becoming the first Black woman to earn a master's
in engineering management. She won many awards for
her teaching.

• • • • •

When a Black woman sets her mind to something, it's next to
impossible to stop her, even if what she's doing means pursuing
a career in a male-dominated field. The world still has some
catching up to do when it comes to Black women holding down
STEM jobs. Few Black females apply for educational programs
in the STEM fields, but it's also easier now than it has ever
been for a Black woman to find success in science, technology,
engineering, or math.

Chapter 3: All-Kinds-of-Awesome Athletes

Women and Girls Who Leveled the Playing Field

Greek mythology tells us of the first female Olympian, Atalanta of Boetia. Born to Schoeneus, she cared not for weaving, the kitchen, or for wasting her precious time with any man who couldn't hold his own against her athletic prowess. Her father, proud of his fleet-footed Boetian babe, disregarded the norms of ancient Greek society and didn't insist on marrying his daughter off for political or financial gain, and supported her decision to marry the man who could outrun her. Her suitors were, however, given a head start, and Atalanta "armed with weapons pursues her naked suitor. If she catches him, he dies." She was outfoxed by Hippomenes, who scattered golden apples as he ran, slowing down the Amazonian runner as she stopped to pick them up. Well matched in every way, they were happy together, even going so far as to desecrate a shrine to Aphrodite by making love on the altar! For this, the Goddess turned Atalanta into a lioness, and she ruled yet again with her wild and regal spirit.

For some Black women athletes like **Althea Gibson** and **Alice Coachman**, competition was a way to blaze a trail. Both athletes were competing at a time when they were still subject to Jim Crow laws in the South, when a woman athlete of any color was an oddity. They paved the way for the future superstars of sports.

• • • • •

When someone tells you that you throw or kick like a girl, I have two words for them: *thank you*. To be told that you throw, kick, punch, or play a sport like a girl is the ultimate compliment because it means you are playing as a top athlete. Throughout history, women and girls have dominated the sports world and proved that "playing like a girl" means being tough, determined, skillful, and talented.

Michelle Carter, gold medalist Olympian, has been to three Olympics and beaten her own record as a shot putter.

Brittney Griner, a professional Women's National Basketball Association player standing tall at six feet, nine inches, was one of the youngest players to get on the 2012 US Olympic women's basketball team finalists roster. She said, "Just knowing you can help somebody out, there's a feeling you can't express."

Women like **Serena** and **Venus Williams**, **Naomi Osaka**, and **Simone Biles** have set the stage for excellence and have proven to be incredible influences for young women around the world.

SIMONE ARIANNE BILES:
She May Be Small, but She Is Mighty

Simone Biles is one of the shortest gymnasts to ever enter the Olympic circuit. Standing tall at a height of four feet, eight inches, one could say that they might have difficulty finding Biles in a large crowd. However, Biles did not let her height become an obstacle. She used her height and body to her advantage and became known for her powerful tumbling in her floor routines. Her dedication and perseverance to push adversity out of the way has earned her the right to be one of the most decorated Olympians in history. She was 2016 Olympic individual all-around, vault, and floor gold medalist and bronze medalist on the beam, and she won five national championships and four world championships. She also has a trick named after her. It is called the Biles, and it consists of a double flip with legs straightened, ending with a half twist. Not only are Simone Biles's accomplishments amazing, but so is her story. She was born to a mother and father who struggled with drug and alcohol addiction. Since her mother and father were unable to care for her and her siblings, Biles, along with her brothers and sisters, were in and out of foster care. However, despite her difficult childhood, her natural talent for gymnastics could not help but shine.

"I'd rather regret the risks that didn't work out than the chances I didn't take at all."

NAOMI OSAKA:
She Spoke Volumes without Even Saying a Word

Naomi Osaka is a tennis legend in the making. At twenty-three years old, this powerhouse of a young woman has won three Grand Slam singles and is the reigning champion at the US Open. As if those accomplishments did not already make her a household name, her activism makes her even more of an inspiration. Osaka made headlines during the last US Open when she wore face masks displaying the names of several Black individuals who had died at the hands of the police. Without even saying a word, her actions spoke loudly about who she is and what she stands for.

"Things have to change."

NICOLE LYNN:
Grid-Iron Greatness

Nicole Lynn became the first Black woman sports agent to represent a top-three pick in the NFL draft: she represented Quinnen Williams in 2019. She studied law at the University of Oklahoma and received her Doctor of Law (JD) degree there. She worked for a time as a financial analyst before turning to the world of sports as a talent rep. She was featured in *Glamour* magazine's 2019 Women of the Year series. In 2020, she received her certification to start representing NBA players. In 2021, Lynn published her autobiography, *Agent You*. Rapper 50 Cent is producing a television series based on her life for Starz. Lynn will be a producer on the series.

ALICE COACHMAN:
Running for Her Life

Boy, could Alice Coachman run and jump! Because of World War II, however, national competitions were as far as an athlete could aspire to in the forties, and the young African American athlete held the national titles for the high jump for twelve consecutive years. Her chance to achieve international recognition finally came in the 1948 Olympics; Coachman was thought to be past her prime, but she decided to go for it anyway. Her teammates lost every race; finally, it was Coachman's turn for the high jump. She took the gold, defeating an opponent who towered above her in height to become, at age twenty-four, the first Black woman to win Olympic gold and the first American woman to go for the gold in track and field.

Coachman was warmly welcomed back to America with an invitation to the White House, a victory motorcade through her home state of Georgia, and a contract to endorse Coca-Cola. Not surprisingly, the racist and sexist America of the forties didn't fully embrace Coachman as it should have. She was, however, lionized in the Black community as a favorite daughter, and truly was the trailblazer for every Black woman athlete to come after her.

ALTHEA GIBSON:
Never Give Up

From the ghetto to the tennis court, Althea Gibson's story is pure SHEroism. At a time when tennis was not only dominated by Whites but by upper-class Whites at that, she managed to serve and volley her way to the top.

Born in 1927 to a Southern sharecropper family, Gibson struggled as a girl with a restless energy that took years for her to channel into positive accomplishments. The family's move to Harlem didn't help. She was bored by school and skipped a lot; teachers and truant officers predicted the worst for Gibson, believing that she was a walking attitude problem whose future lay as far as the nearest reform school.

Although things looked dire for Gibson, she had a thing or two to show the naysayers. Like many SHEroes, Gibson had to bottom out before she could get to the top. She dropped out of school and drifted from job to job until, at only fourteen, she found herself a ward of New York City's welfare department. This turned out to be the best thing that could have happened to Gibson—a wise welfare worker not only helped her find steady work but also enrolled her into New York's police sports program. Gibson fell in love with paddle ball, and upon graduating to real tennis, amazed everyone with her natural ability The New York Cosmopolitan Club, an interracial sports and social organization, sponsored the teen and arranged for her to have a tennis coach, Fred Johnson. Gibson's transformation from "bad girl" to tennis sensation was immediate; she won the New York State Open Championship one year later. She captured the attention of two wealthy patrons who agreed to sponsor her if she finished high school. She did in 1949—and went on to accept a tennis scholarship to Florida Agricultural and Mechanical University.

Gibson's battles weren't over yet, though. She aced nine straight Negro national championships and chafed at her exclusion from tournaments closed to non-White players. Fighting hard to compete with White players, Gibson handled herself well, despite being exposed to racism at its most heinous. Her dignified struggle to overcome segregation in tennis won her many supporters of all colors. Finally, one of her biggest fans and admirers, the editor of *American Lawn and Tennis* magazine, wrote an article decrying the "color barrier" in tennis. The walls came

down. By 1958, Althea Gibson won the singles and doubles at Wimbledon and twice took the US national championships at the US Open as well.

Then, citing money woes, she retired; she just couldn't make a living at women's tennis. She took up golf, becoming the first Black woman to qualify for the Ladies Professional Golf Association. But she never excelled in golf as she had in tennis, and in the seventies and eighties she returned to the game she truly loved, serving as a mentor and coach to an up-and-coming generation of African American women tennis players.

Through sheer excellence and a willingness to work on behalf of her race, Althea Gibson made a huge difference in the sports world, for which we are all indebted to her.

WILMA RUDOLPH:
La Gazelle

Runner Wilma Rudolph's life is the story of a great spirit and heart overcoming obstacles that would have stopped anyone else in their tracks, literally! Born in Bethlehem, Tennessee, in 1955, Rudolph contracted polio at the age of four and was left with a useless leg.

Rudolph's family was in dire straits with a total of eighteen children from her father's two marriages. Both parents worked constantly to feed the burgeoning brood, her father as a porter and her mother as a house cleaner, and it was more important to feed Rudolph and her siblings than it was to get the medical attention Rudolph needed to recover the use of her leg. Two years later, circumstances eased a bit, and at the age of six she started riding the back of the bus with her mother to Nashville twice a week for physical therapy. Although doctors predicted she would never walk without braces, Rudolph kept up her rehabilitation program for five years, and not only did the braces come off but "by the time I was twelve," she told the *Chicago Tribune*, "I was challenging every boy in the neighborhood at running, jumping, everything."

Her exceptional ability didn't go unnoticed. A coach with Tennessee State University saw how she was winning every race she entered in high school and offered to train her for the Olympics, which Rudolph hadn't even heard of. Nevertheless, she qualified for the Olympics at sixteen and took home a bronze medal in the 1956 Summer Games for the 100-meter relay. Still in high school, she decided to work toward a gold medal for the 1960 games.

Well, she did that and more. The three gold medals she won in the 1960 Olympics in Rome—in the 100-meter dash, the 200-meter dash, and the 4 x 100 relay—turned her into a superstar overnight. Rudolph was the first American woman ever to win triple gold in a single Olympics. People were stumbling over each other to find the superlatives to describe her. The French named her "La Gazelle," and in America she was known as "The Fastest Woman on Earth." Rudolph was everybody's darling after that, with invitations to the JFK White House and numerous guest appearances on television. The flip side of all the glory, however, was that Rudolph received hardly any financial reward for her public appearances and had to work odd jobs to get through college.

One year later, Rudolph again set the world on fire by breaking the record for the 100-meter dash: 11.2 seconds. Unpredictably, she sat out the '64 Olympic Games and stayed in school, graduating with a degree in education and returning to the very school she had attended as a youngster to teach second grade. In 1967, she worked for the Job Corps and Operation Champion, a program that endeavored to bring star athletes into American ghettos as positive role models for young kids. Rudolph herself loved to talk to kids about sports and was a powerful symbol with her inspiring story.

That Wilma Rudolph touched the lives of children is best evidenced in a letter-writing campaign taken up by a class of fourth graders in Jessup, Maryland, who requested the *World Book Encyclopedia* correct their error in excluding the world-class athlete. The publisher complied immediately! Rudolph has also been honored with induction into both the Olympic Hall of Fame and the National Track and Field Hall of Fame. A film version of her autobiography *Wilma*, starring Cicely Tyson, was produced to tremendous acclaim. Her death from terminal brain cancer took place shortly after she received an honor as one of "the Great Ones" at the premiere National Sports Awards in 1993.

"I have spent a lifetime trying to share what it has meant to be a woman first in the world of sports so that other young women will have a chance to reach their dreams."

EVELYN ASHFORD:
The Power of Persistence

"[Wilma Rudolph] inspired me to pursue my dream of being a runner, to stick with it," said runner Evelyn Ashford, whose incredible athletic staying power in a sport with a high burnout rate was notable. She participated in Olympic games for nearly twenty years, returning to pick up a gold medal in 1992 as a thirty-five-year-old mother of one. Ashford was always gifted at sports, but never took herself seriously until a male coach noticed her speed and issued a challenge for her to race his male track team. When she beat the "best guy" on the field, Ashford suddenly got the attention and positive support that spurred her on.

By 1975, she had earned a full scholarship to UCLA. One year later, she was a member of the Olympic team, but had to wait for the next games four years later to make her mark. In 1980, in protest of the Soviet Union's invasion of Afghanistan, President Carter made the choice to boycott the Summer Olympic Games. Along with her peers, Evelyn Ashford's chances to win were dashed. But her persistence paid off in spades; she came back after the terrible disappointment and won a gold medal for the 100-meter sprint and another gold medal for the 400-meter relay in the 1984 Summer Olympic Games held in Los Angeles. Renowned as the perfect model of a good sport both on and off the field, she takes enormous joy in running with fellow champions Alice Brown, Sheila Echols, and Florence Griffith-Joyner and promoting track and field as a sport. There's no doubt that Wilma Rudolph would be proud of Evelyn Ashford's accomplishments.

JACKIE JOYNER-KERSEE:
Queen of the Field

Arguably the greatest cross-category track-and-field star of all time, Jackie Joyner-Kersee has a string of firsts to her credit, and keeps racking them up at an astonishing rate: she was the first US woman to win gold for the long jump, the first woman ever to exceed 7,000 points for the heptathlon, and the first athlete, man or woman, to win multiple gold medals in both single and multiple events in track and field. Since her debut in the 1984 Los Angeles Summer Events, Joyner-Kersee remained at the top of her game.

Along with her athletic prowess, Joyner-Kersee's charisma and style made her an overnight sensation. In addition, she has a policy of giving back as good as she gets to the community she's from. She has a strong desire to nurture athleticism and scholarship in urban settings where access to a place to run and play is the first of many challenges underprivileged kids face. Her foundation, the Jackie Joyner-Kersee Youth Center Foundation, developed a recreational and educational facility for kids in

East St. Louis where area kids have access to a computer lab, library, ball fields, basketball courts, and, of course, indoor and outdoor tracks.

Like several other outstanding athletes, Joyner-Kersee comes from poverty, an alum of the poorest part of East St. Louis. Fortunately, she received encouragement from her family to participate in sports. She discovered track and field at the Mayor Brown Community Center, and her Olympic dreams started when she saw the 1976 Olympics on television. Joyner-Kersee quickly emerged as a veritable "sporting savant" and started breaking national records at fourteen, excelling at basketball and volleyball while maintaining a super grade point average. Soon she was courted by many tantalizing college scholarships, ultimately deciding to attend UCLA, where Bob Kersee would be her coach.

Bob Kersee, who she married in 1986, convinced both Jackie and the powers-that-be at UCLA that her career lay in multi-track events. Looking back, it's hard to imagine Joyner-Kersee competing in any other event than the one she is the best in the world at. Her forte is the seven-event heptathlon, a previously overlooked event in which athletes earn points by running a 200-meter dash, competing in both high and long jumps, throwing both the javelin and shot put, running the 100-meter hurdles, and completing an 800-meter run, all in two days. These herculean challenges alone call for super-SHEroism, and Jackie not only made the heptathlon her own but through her prowess made the event a track-and-field favorite.

At the time, she was one of the few African American athletes to get prestigious product endorsement contracts and was very aware of her opportunity to serve as a positive role model, telling *Women's Sports & Fitness*, "I feel that as an African American woman the only thing I can do is continue to better myself, continue to perform well, continue to make sure that I'm a good commodity. If doors aren't opened for me, then maybe it will happen for someone else."

"I understand the position I am in, but I also know that tomorrow there's going to be someone else. So I try to keep things in perspective."

FLORENCE GRIFFITH JOYNER:
Going With the Flo-Jo

Jackie Joyner-Kersee's brother, Al Joyner, was an Olympic athlete too. When he met the flamboyant Florence Griffith in 1984, the runner who made her mark on the track world as much for her long fingernails and colorful attire as for being "the world's fastest woman," she was working days as a customer service rep for a bank and moonlighting as a beautician at night. The former world-class runner had lost the gold to Valerie Brisco in 1980 and had given up. At Al's urging, she began training again. They also started dating seriously and got married soon after. This time, Florence had the will to win and stormed the 1988 Seoul Olympics to take home three gold medals. Off the track, "Flo-Jo," as the press dubbed her, devoted herself to working with children, hoping to educate the youth of America to "reach beyond their dreams," eat right, play sports, and stay away from drugs. After her record-setting gold medal races in Seoul, *Ms.* enthused, "Florence Griffith Joyner has joined the immortals, rising to their status on the force of her amazing athletic achievement, aided by the singular nature of her personality and approach."

"Looking good is almost as important as running well. It's part of feeling good about myself."

A FEW OF THE FIRSTS IN WOMEN'S SPORTS

Lucy Diggs Slowe became the first Black American woman to win a major sports title at the very first American Tennis Association tournament. She was also the first Black American woman to serve as a dean of women at an American university.

Cardte Hicks was the first Black American drafted to play professional basketball, and the first woman to dunk in a professional game. She did it in Holland during a *professional men's* game.

Serena Williams became the first tennis player to win twenty-three Grand Slam singles titles in the Open Era.

Gabby Douglas was born in Virginia on December 31, 1995. She is the very first African American to win the Olympic individual all-around title. She took gold at both the 2012 and 2016 Summer Olympics as well. She had her very first experience with gymnastics when she was three years old, when her older sister showed her how to do a cartwheel. Soon after learning the cartwheel, Gabby learned how to do a one-handed cartwheel on her own, and thus her love for gymnastics was born.

At Dover International Speedway, **Brehanna Daniels** became the first Black American woman to pit a car in a national NASCAR race.

MO'NE DAVIS:
Because I Am a Girl

Mo'ne Davis has been a champion of girls' sports since she was thirteen, fighting to create more space for young girls and to reform students' sports by working to close the gender gap. From a young age she excelled in sports, playing basketball, soccer, and baseball. In 2014, she played in the Little League World Series and even pitched a winning game. This made her not only the first African American girl to play in the Little League World Series but also the first *girl* to ever pitch a shutout and earn a win at the series. Davis collaborated with M4D3 to create her own line of sneakers and donated some of the proceeds to the Because I Am a Girl initiative, which helps raise millions of girls in developing nations out of poverty. She was the youngest athlete to get a feature on the cover of *Sports Illustrated*, and received praise from numerous important public figures, including Michelle Obama.

"I just try to be myself. I hope I encourage
people just to be themselves, no matter
what happens."

MAYA MOORE:
A True Baller

Maya Moore is a professional basketball superstar turned reformer. She sat out this past season, and will continue to sit out, to focus on a passion other than the game: criminal justice reform. After hearing about the case of Jonathan Irons, a man she believed to be wrongfully accused, she decided to work with him to learn about and push for change. While her dominating presence is missed in the WNBA and on Team USA, her decision is supported and understood. She participates in interviews and panels about her goal to see the prison system reformed, especially regarding its treatment of minorities. Moore has shifted from being a playmaker to a change-maker.

"I'm here because I care."

• • • • •

Black women athletes fly in the face of a history in which Black women had little agency over their own bodies. They are strong, powerful, and prove themselves in competition time and time again. Not content to take a bench-warming session, these amazing athletes are breaking records and reshaping our notions of athleticism. Not everyone is equipped to become a Venus or Serena Williams, sure, but Black female athletes empower Black women everywhere with their mere presence on the stage. They stand as defiant examples of determination and hard work, and let the world know the body is a sacred space.

Chapter 4: Unbought and Unbossed

Black Women Fighting for Equality and Social Justice

Whether they took a stand by keeping their seat or faced brutal repercussions for fighting for equality, Black women have always been at the vanguard of social justice. Far from a male-dominated arena, the fight for equality takes both genders working in unison to find any measure of success. Brave Black women led the way and continue to champion equality where there is disparity. Their continuing struggle for rights is a battle we should all be involved in because their fight ensures rights for all.

ROSA PARKS:
The First Lady of Civil Rights

Rosa Parks gave a human face to the civil rights movement. She showed how the issues addressed in all the speeches affected a woman's life on an ordinary day. The woman was Rosa Louise McCauley Parks; the day became an extraordinary one that rocked the nation and changed history.

Parks often walked home from work to avoid the "back of the bus" issue, until December 1, 1955, when she was returning home from a long day of sewing at a Montgomery department store. The buses from downtown were always fairly crowded and had a section designated for Black people behind the ten rows of seats in the front for White folks. Parks was sitting in the first row of the "blacks only" section when the White section filled up, leaving a White man without a seat. The tacit understanding was that, in such a scenario, the Black person was supposed to stand and let the White person have the seat. The White bus driver called for the four Black people in the front row of the Black section to get up and let the White man have the row. Parks refused and the driver called the police.

Though there had been several incidents on Montgomery buses, Parks stuck to her guns and became the pivotal legal case for the burgeoning civil rights movement's attack on segregated seating. Her solitary action started a firestorm of controversy, including a bus boycott

and protest march led by Martin Luther King Jr. and Coretta Scott King. Rosa Parks's courage in that split-second moment when she made her decision is at the very crux of the African American struggle for equality. The US District Court eventually ruled segregated seating to be unconstitutional.

In 1980, Parks was honored by *Ebony* magazine as "the living black woman who had done the most to advance the cause of civil rights."

"You didn't have to wait for a lynching. You died a little each time you found yourself face to face with this kind of discrimination."

HARRIET TUBMAN:
Harriet the Spy (Not Kidding)

In her day, Harriet Tubman was lovingly referred to as Moses for leading her people home to freedom. An escaped slave herself, she pulled off feat after amazing feat and gave freedom to many who would otherwise have never known it. Harriet Tubman was a "conductor" on the Underground Railroad, perhaps the best there ever was. She is best known for this activity, but she was also a feminist, a nurse, and for a time, a spy. Her keenest interest was social reform, both for her gender and her people.

Born around 1821 on a plantation in Maryland, Tubman struggled with grand mal seizures after a blow to the head as a child, but the damage from a severely fractured skull didn't stop her from the most dangerous work she could have possibly undertaken: taking groups of slaves to freedom in the North. During her slow recovery from being hit in the head with a two-pound weight by an overseer, she began praying and contemplating the enslavement of Black people, resolving to do what she could, with faith in a higher power. She married John Tubman, a free man, in 1844, and lived in fear that she would be sold into the Deep South. When she heard rumors that she was about to be sold, she plotted her escape, begging John to come with her. He not only refused but threatened to turn her in.

Tubman escaped to freedom by herself, but immediately plotted to return for her family members using the Underground Railroad. She ultimately rescued all her family members except John; he had taken a new wife and remained behind. She led more than two hundred slaves to safety and freedom, encouraging her "passengers" with gospel songs sung in a deep, strong voice. She also developed a code to signal danger using biblical quotations and certain songs. Harriet Tubman always outfoxed the White people who questioned her about the groups of Black people traveling with her. She lived in constant threat of hanging, with a $40,000 price on her head and many close calls. One of the most dramatic incidents that shows Tubman's resourcefulness and resolve occurred when she bought tickets heading South to evade White people demanding to know what a group of Black people were doing traveling together. She always carried a gun to dissuade any frightened fugitives from turning tail. "You'll be free or die," she told them—and she never lost a passenger.

Tubman also started connecting with abolitionists in the North, developing a strong admiration for John Brown (she conspired with him in his raid at Harper's Ferry) and Susan B. Anthony. During the Civil War, she nursed Black soldiers, worked as a spy for the Union, and even led a raid that freed 750 slaves. After the war, she lived in Auburn, New York, in a house that had been a way station for the Underground Railroad, teaching Black people how to cope with newfound freedom, gathering food, clothing, and money for poor Black people, and founding a home for elderly and indigent Black people. Tubman's last years were spent in abject poverty

Harriet Tubman

despite all she had given to others, but she died at the age of ninety-three having accomplished the task she set herself as a girl. She was the great emancipator, offering her people hope, freedom, and new beginnings. Reformer and writer Thomas Wentworth Higginson named her "the greatest heroine of the age."

"When I found I had crossed that line, I looked
to my hands to see if I was the same person.
There was such a glory over everything."

DAISY BATES:
Fighting the System and Winning!

Daisy Bates was one of the first civil rights warriors called into action in the fight for desegregation. Together with her husband, L.C. Bates, a Black man who had been educated as a journalist, she took over a Little Rock newspaper, the *Arkansas State Press*, and turned it into a platform for "the people," reporting crimes committed against Black people that the White papers ignored. Daisy worked as a reporter, covering with complete honesty, for example, the cold-blooded murder of a Black soldier by military police. The White business community was outraged over the *State Press*'s coverage: They feared the army would leave their town and withdraw all advertising. However, the Bateses' brave courage in the face of brutality toward Black people curtailed these crimes, and Little Rock became a more liberated town despite itself.

Then the movement toward desegregation heated up, with Daisy Bates right in the thick of things. The Supreme Court had declared segregation of schools unconstitutional in May of 1954, giving Southern schools the chance to describe how and when they would make the required changes. The local school board had responded by saying that they would take on the notion of integration "gradually." Little Rock's Black community was up in arms about the foot-dragging, and after butting their heads in many stony-faced meetings with the school board, they opted to take matters into their own hands. The state and local NAACP chapters decided that they would try to enroll the students into the segregated schools and build up cases of denied admissions in order to create a true challenge to the policy of gradualism. Daisy Bates, as president of the NAACP in Little Rock, worked with the *State Press* and other papers to publicize this flouting of the Supreme Court's ruling. Finally, in 1957, they decided to integrate the high school come hell or high water. The children who would put their bodies on the line would become famous overnight as "Daisy's children," and suffered personal agony for the cause of racial injustice.

When nine children were selected to attend "Whites only" Central High School, Daisy acted as their escort and protector. Answering a poll screened by school officials, the group of young heroes and SHEroes consisted of: Carlotta Walls, Thelma Mothershed, Melba Pattillo, Ernest Green, Terrence Roberts, Gloria Ray, Minnijean Brown, Jefferson Thomas, and Elizabeth Eckford. When Little Rock school superintendent Virgil Blossom decreed that no adults could accompany the Black students, Daisy called all of their homes and told them there would be a change of plans.

Elizabeth Eckford's family had no telephone, so she showed up on opening day only to be faced by an angry White mob that also attacked the reporters and photographers. The mob siege lasted seventeen days, until one thousand paratroopers showed up in response to orders from the White House to carry through the order of legal integration of the school.

However, the students were on their own once inside, prey to taunts, shoving, and threats of violence. Daisy Bates continued to protect and advise the children throughout the ordeal, accompanying them to every meeting with a school official when racial incidents happened. The struggle at Little Rock was only the first in a round of actions that ultimately led to full legal desegregation. Though difficult, the victory was entirely due to Daisy and her "children," who showed the nation that you could stand up to hatred and ignorance with honesty and dignity. You can fight a losing battle and win.

"No man or woman who tries to pursue an ideal in his or her own way is without enemies."

CLAUDETTE COLVIN:
Taking a Stand by Taking a Seat

Several months prior to the arrest of Rosa Parks, Montgomery-born Claudette Colvin, a fifteen-year-old high school student, refused to give up her own seat on a segregated bus on a ride home from school and was arrested. She would later become one of four female plaintiffs in *Browder v. Gayle,* a Supreme Court case that resulted in the desegregation of busses in Montgomery and Alabama.

"I knew then and I know now, when it comes to justice, there is no easy way to get it."

UNITA BLACKWELL:
Why Your Vote Really Counts

Unita Blackwell was a civil rights activist. In June 1964, two activists from the Student Nonviolent Coordinating Committee traveled to Mayersville, Mississippi, and spoke at Blackwell's church about registering to vote. The next week, Blackwell and a group of seven other people went to the town hall to try to register. A group of White men tried to scare them off, and only two of the people who went were allowed to take the literacy test the town required of registered voters. To make matters worse, the next day, Blackwell and her husband were fired from their jobs for trying to register to vote. But none of that kept Blackwell from registering. It took her three tries, but she was finally allowed to take the voter registration test. Later, Blackwell was the first Black person to be elected mayor of a town in the state of Mississippi.

PATRISSE CULLORS:
#BlackLivesMatter

Patrisse Cullors is a community activist, writer, and artist. In 2013, Cullors, along with activists Alicia Garza and Opal Tometi, created the Black Lives Matter movement. Cullors created the hashtag "#blacklivesmatter" to spread the word about the movement. She continues to advocate for an end to police violence, inspired in part by her brother's experiences with police brutality within the detention system. Cullors is

especially passionate about fighting for Black queer rights.
She has received many awards and was also awarded
honorary doctorates from Chicago's South Shore International
College and Clarkson University. In 2018, Cullors released her
memoir, *When They Call You a Terrorist: A Black Lives
Matter Memoir.*

BLACK
LIVES
MATTER

SHIRLEY CHISHOLM:
"Unbought and Unbossed"

Shirley Chisholm was a nonstop SHEro whose own sense of empowerment spread to everyone who met her. In 1968, Chisholm was the first Black woman to be elected to Congress, a historic triumph for her gender and race. Four years later, she ran for president in the primaries.

Born in the borough of Brooklyn, New York, in 1924, she spent seven years in Barbados with her grandmother, Emily Seale. She credits the "stiff upper lip" yet excellent education she received in Barbados for giving her an advantage when she returned to the United States. Chisholm garnered many scholarship offers upon her graduation from high school, choosing Brooklyn College to study psychology and Spanish with the intention of becoming a teacher. She got involved with the Harriet Tubman Society, where she developed a keen sense of Black pride. Acing every course, she received a lot of encouragement to "do something" with her life. A White political science professor urged her to pursue politics, a daunting idea at the time, but the seed was planted.

After an arduous job search, Chisholm finally found work at the Mount Cavalry Child Center; her magna cum laude degree didn't seem to offset her color for many potential employers. She also took night classes at Columbia, where she met Conrad Chisholm. They married soon after, giving her a stable foundation upon which to build her house of dreams. She continued to work in early childhood education,

becoming director of several day care centers and
private schools.

In the sixties, Chisholm stepped into the political arena,
campaigning for a seat in the state assembly in her district.
She won the Democratic seat in 1964 and began the first
step in a history-making career, winning again in '65 and '66.
Then she decided to run for the US Assembly. Even though
she was up against a much more experienced candidate
with deep-pocketed financial backing, Chisholm prevailed;
she was aware that there were thirteen thousand more
women than men in the district, and quickly mobilized the
female vote. She also underwent surgery for a tumor at this
time, but went back to work immediately, quickly earning a
reputation as one of the most hard-charging Black members
of the assembly.

Even in Congress, the race issue reared its head. She was
assigned to the Agricultural Committee to work with
food stamp distribution because she was a Black woman.
Chisholm didn't take this lying down, and fought to get off
that committee, moving on to Veteran's Affairs and, finally,
Education and Labor, where she believed she could really
do some good. Known for her straight-shooting verbal style
and maverick political ways, she always saw herself as an
advocate for her constituency, seeking to be the voice of
those traditionally overlooked by politics: Hispanics, Native
Americans, drug addicts, and gay activists.

As a presidential candidate for the 1972 Democratic
nomination, she placed women's rights at the center of her
campaign, claiming that she was not a "gimmick" candidate

but a serious contender. Although she failed to get the nod, it did make her a national spokesperson for the civil and women's rights movements. Since then, she helped create the National Political Congress of Black Women, and taught, lectured, and authored two books, *Unbought and Unbossed* and *The Good Fight*. Shirley Chisholm was at the forefront of the fight to obtain real political power for African American woman.

"I'm the only one among you who has the balls to run for president."

FANNIE LOU HAMER:
Bravery Unbound

Fannie Lou Hamer grew up a sharecropper's daughter in Montgomery, Mississippi, where she was exposed to the worst face of racial injustice. Forced to quit school in the sixth grade to work in the cotton fields in order to help support her family, she got involved in the effort to register Black people to vote in 1962. At the time, a literacy test was required in order to secure the right to vote, and Hamer helped teach people so they could pass the test. One day, Hamer was on a bus with a group of fellow African American youths who were challenging the "Whites only" policy at the bus terminal diner. When they were attacked by state troopers called in to deal with the "insurrection," Hamer was hurt badly and jailed with everyone else from the bus. Her sufferings had only begun, though. Hamer was incarcerated in a cell with two Black men who were ordered to beat her with a metal-spiked, leather billy club. Hamer was permanently blinded in one eye by this beating and suffered kidney damage, but she emerged with even more inner resolve to put an end to racial injustice. Hamer worked without cessation for many related causes: for Head Start for Black schools, jobs for poor Black people, and against the Vietnam War because she felt Black soldiers were being sent to protect rights they themselves didn't have at home. Fannie Hamer risked her life over and over to improve the lot of her people until her death in 1977, never receiving the attention that was her due. A true unsung SHEro, her essential belief was that "we serve God by serving our fellow [human beings]."

ESLANDA GOODE ROBESON:
"Africans Are People"

The daughter of a freed slave, Eslanda Goode Robeson distinguished herself both in political activism and as an anthropologist.

Robeson, born in 1896, was passionately interested in Africa and the conditions that made the mother continent vulnerable. Her mother, Eslanda Cardoza Goode, was of mixed race, born among South Carolina's free Black people to a mixed-race mother and a wealthy Jewish Spaniard, Isaac Nunez Cardoza. Her uncle Francis Louis Cardoza was named "the most highly educated Negro in America" by Henry Ward Beecher. When she was six, her father died of alcohol abuse and the family moved to New York City just in time for the birth of the Harlem Renaissance. Robeson was well educated herself, attending Teachers College at Columbia University and one year of medical school, ultimately receiving her degree in chemistry from Columbia. Her other interests included a strong proclivity for politics and the desire to fight for racial equality. Robeson was on her way to becoming a model for the new equality when she became the first Black person to work in the pathology and surgery departments of Columbia Presbyterian, where she ran the lab. In the twenties, she met and married Paul Robeson; after hearing him sing at a party, she became convinced he had a future in show business. She talked him into performing and soon his career was launched. By the mid-twenties, Paul was the toast of Europe and America. Robeson quit her job to travel with Paul and manage his career. However, over and over the duo suffered the sickening hypocrisy of a White society that lauded Paul as a champion of stage and screen while not allowing he and Robeson to eat in the same restaurants as the White music patrons. To avoid the pain, Robeson began to stay home and focus on their shared dream of a modern Black family—emancipated, educated, and enlightened.

In the thirties, the ever intellectually restless Robeson developed an intense interest in anthropology and in Africa. Studying at London University and the London School of Economics, she became even more radicalized: "I soon became fed up with white students and teachers 'interpreting' the Negro mind and character to me," she wrote later. "Especially when I felt, as I did very often, that their interpretation was wrong."

She decided to make her own conclusions. She traveled to
Africa several times, exploring widely, up the Congo and into
the heartland by any means available. Her exploration led her
to emphasize the importance of racial pride in overcoming
racism, and she banded with other Black people to found
the Council of African Affairs. She was always extremely
outspoken about the plight of her people as a result of slavery
and colonialism, and never backed down from a debate. She
drew fire when she suggested the Soviet Union had created
a better foundation for equality than the United States. In
the forties, during World War II, she was especially vocal,
perceiving that the war against fascism was an opportunity
for a more racially united and equal-opportunity America.
Her book *African Journey* was published in 1945; that same
year, as a representative of the Council on African Affairs,
Robeson participated in the conference that founded the
United Nations.

In the fifties, the activity and views of the Robesons were
brought to the attention of Senator Joseph McCarthy,
who called her before the House Un-American Activities
Committee. McCarthy was no match for the brilliance and
verbal dexterity of Robeson, who turned the tables on him,
drilling him with questions about the Black civil rights issue.
But McCarthy got his revenge, revoking both their passports,
reducing Paul's income from international concert tours to
almost nil.

This only spurred Robeson on to greater activism—ultimately
her passport was reinstated, and she traveled to Germany
to receive the Peace Medal and the Clara Zetkin Medal, a
governmental award for women who have fought for world

peace. She continued to write articles and give speeches in support of equality and justice until she died in 1965. No matter what the personal cost, Robeson fought to free her people from the invisible bonds that still held them back. Her work was invaluable in the civil rights movement; her call for absolute racial quality rang clear and true: "No man can be free until all men are free."

CORETTA SCOTT KING:
Unshakable Faith

Like the Robesons, the Kings had a marriage based on love—for each other and for racial equality. After the assassination of Martin Luther King Jr., Coretta Scott King gained recognition in her own right as a pillar of the civil rights movement. A talented musician, King was born in Alabama in 1927 and was educated at Antioch, where she got a degree in music and elementary education and was exposed to White people in a very different environment than the South, learning a great deal about techniques to foster interracial communication. In 1953, she married Martin Luther King Jr. while they were both college students, and they pursued a life together: her music—she got a higher degree at the New England Conservatory of Music—and his theological degree. Coming from a long line of ministers, Martin felt a call to become a pastor, a decision that found the young couple moving to Montgomery, Alabama, after their education. They had their first of four children in their first year at the Dexter Avenue Baptist Church and became deeply involved in the actions of the civil rights movement. Martin Luther King Jr. led the bus boycott after Rosa Parks's historic bus ride. As the footage shows, King was right beside her husband at every protest, fighting for the rights of all African Americans. She also participated in fundraising for the movement by giving more than thirty concerts in Europe and the United States to raise money for Martin's organization, the Southern Christian Leadership Conference (SCLC).

The Kings traveled extensively in their work—to Ghana, to India, to Nigeria, and in 1964, to Norway to receive Dr. King's Nobel Peace Prize. Four years later, the world watched in horror as Martin was gunned down in Memphis, Tennessee, during a garbage workers' strike. King didn't shrink from the work at hand and led a protest in Memphis four days later with her children at her side. Her quiet dignity captured the nation; that year she was voted Woman of the Year and Most Admired Woman by college students.

From that fateful day, King stepped forward and took up the mantle of leadership in the civil rights movement, which she shared with the young Jesse Jackson. She amazed everyone with her stamina and heart as she made speech after speech and led march after march. She has received innumerable awards for her tireless efforts in her lifetime. She founded the Martin Luther King Jr. Center for Nonviolent Change and has also led the attention of the nation in new directions, organizing anti-war protests, antinuclear and anti-apartheid lobbies and employment for African Americans. More than one hundred colleges have given her honorary doctorates. Coretta Scott King has never hesitated to give herself to the struggle for freedom and justice, viewing it as both "a privilege" and "a blessing."

GEORGIA GILMORE:
Making History Happen

Georgia Gilmore grew up in Montgomery, Alabama during, the time of the civil rights movement—a time when Black people were only seen for the color of their skin. Every day when she took the bus to work, she was forced to sit in the back. She eventually grew tired of paying money to and financially supporting a discriminatory system. This eventually inspired her to join the Montgomery bus boycott. However, finding alternate means of transportation for everyone in town cost money. Thankfully, Gilmore was an amazing cook! So during the boycott meetings, she would sell food to help fund the repairs that needed to be made and vehicles that needed to be purchased. Georgia Gilmore was the girl behind the scenes and helped make the Montgomery bus boycott happen!

> "We felt that we had accomplished something that no one ever thought would ever happen in the city of Montgomery."

SOJOURNER TRUTH:
"Ain't I a Woman?"

Sojourner Truth's name alone suggests SHEroism. It fits her perfectly—she was a fire-breathing preacher, suffragist, and vigilant abolitionist. Unschooled and born to slavery, she didn't allow these disadvantages to prevent her from becoming one of the most charismatic and powerful orators of the nineteenth century. In fact, like many African Americans of the day, hardship seemed to make her only stronger, like a blade forged by fire.

She hailed from Dutch country in upstate New York and grew up speaking Dutch. Christened Isabella, she was sold away from her parents as a child and was traded many times, until finally landing with John Dumont for whom she worked for sixteen years. At fourteen, she was given to an older slave to be his wife and bore five children. In 1826, one year before she was to be legally freed, Isabella ran away from Dumont and hid with a pacifist Quaker family.

Upon hearing that one of her sons had been sold into lifetime slavery in Alabama, Isabella sued over this illegal sale of her son and, remarkably, won the case. Isabella moved to New York in the 1830s and worked as a maid for a religious community, the Magdalenes, whose mission was the conversion of prostitutes to Christianity.

By 1843, the extremely religious Isabella heard a calling to become a traveling preacher. She renamed herself Sojourner Truth and hit the road, where her talent for talking amazed all who heard her at revivals, camp meetings, churches, and on the side of the road if the occasion arose. She kept her sermons to the simple themes of brotherly love and tolerance. In Massachusetts, Truth encountered liberals who enlightened her on the topics of feminism and abolition. Her autobiography, as told to the antislavery forerunner William Lloyd Garrison, provided a powerful weapon for the cause of abolition when published. Her story, *The Narrative of Sojourner Truth*, was one of the first stories of a woman slave to be widely known, and was retold many times, including the charmingly entitled version "Sojourner Truth, the Libyan Sibyl," by Harriet Beecher Stowe, which was published by the *Atlantic Monthly*.

Truth then put her religious fervor into the message of abolition, a holy mission into which she threw all her formidable will and energy. Her call to end the slavery of human beings in this country was powerful. There is a beloved story showing her quick tongue and even quicker mind and spirit: when the great Frederick Douglass openly doubted there could be an end to slavery without the spilling of blood, in a flash she replied, "Frederick, is God dead?"

By the middle of the nineteenth century, Truth was preaching the twin messages of abolition and women's suffrage. She was unwavering in her convictions and made the eloquent point that "if colored men get their rights and not colored women, colored men will be masters over the women, and it will be just as bad as before." She threw herself into the Civil War effort, helping runaway slaves and Black soldiers. President Lincoln was so impressed with the legend of Sojourner Truth that he invited her to the White House to talk.

Sojourner Truth worked, preached, and fought right up to her dying day in 1883. She lived long enough to see one of her fondest hopes—the abolition of slavery—be realized, and along with the estimable Harriet Tubman, is one of the two most respected African American women of the nineteenth century. Was she a woman? Yes, indeed. And a SHEro for all time!

"I have ploughed, and planted, and gathered into barns, and no man could head me! And ain't I a woman?"

DOROTHY HEIGHT:
She Had a Dream Too

Dorothy Height was civil rights activist who focused on the issues of equality for Black Americans and for women. She was one of the first to see the two issues as one systemic problem and to address them both equally. Through her work with the National

Council of Negro Women and the Young Women's Christian Association, Height became a leading figure in the civil rights movement and regularly worked with its leaders including John Lewis and Dr. Martin Luther King Jr. She helped organize the March on Washington and sat within arms' length of Dr. King when he gave his "I have a Dream" speech. In 1971, she helped cofound the National Women's Political Caucus with Gloria Steinem, Shirley Chisholm, and Betty Friedan. For her years of service in civil rights, Height was awarded the Presidential Medal of Freedom in 1994. In 2004, she was awarded the Congressional Gold Medal.

YOLANDA KING AND ATTALLAH SHABAZZ:
Passing On the Torch

The daughters of two very different civil rights warriors, Martin Luther King Jr. and Malcolm X, have recently paired up to represent the next generation of activism. Although Yolanda King and Attallah (Arabic for "gift of god") Shabazz were raised in different faiths and come from different philosophical points of view, their commonalities override their dissimilarities. Both lost their fathers to assassins as children under the public eye, and both desired to escape that attention and live their own lives. King and Shabazz grew into two creative spirits for whom the arts provide release, solace, and strength. They were wary of each other upon meeting in New York City, where they were both trying to start acting careers. It wasn't long, however, before a bond was forged and they started working on a play together, *Stepping into Tomorrow*, a musical dramedy with a powerful message of empowerment for youth. The play began a career of collaboration and activism in which they both travel extensively lecturing on civil rights, the importance of the arts, and the legacy of their fathers. In Yolanda King's words, "I see these responsibilities not as a burden, but as an extension of who I am."

TARANA BURKE:
#MeToo

In 2017, the "MeToo" hashtag went viral and Tarana Burke emerged as a leading voice in the discussion surrounding sexual assault. In 2018, she founded Me Too International, a global nonprofit organization that works with both mainstream and grassroots organizations to address the situations that lead to widespread sexual assault. Burke has been named the 2017 *TIME* magazine Person of the Year and one of the magazine's "100 Most Influential People." She was awarded the 2019 Sydney Peace Prize and the Harvard Gleitsman Citizen Activist Award. She is currently the senior director of Girls for Gender Equity in Brooklyn, New York, an organization that empowers Black girls through various programs and classes.

"Get up. Stand Up. Speak up. Do something."

WANGARI MAATHAI:
Green Goddess

Early on, Wangari Maathai was instructed by her mother about the importance and sanctity of land and that which grows upon it, especially trees. She set her sights on saving the farmlands, forests, and grasslands of Africa. On World Environment Day in 1977, she and her supporters planted seven trees in a public park and laid the foundation for the Green Belt movement. "We wanted to emphasize that by cutting trees, removing vegetation, having this soil erosion, we were literally stripping the Earth of its color," she remarked. Maathai discovered that only 3 percent of the Kenyan forest was still standing. As a result, Kenyan villagers were suffering malnutrition, erosion of their farmland, and the subsequent loss of water as springs and creeks dried up. She quite accurately foresaw famine and environmental disaster unless trees were again planted to restore the environment to its natural state. Maathai traveled throughout Kenya, teaching village women how to plant trees and how to start them from seeds they collected. Soon children got involved in the Green Belt planting projects, and by 1988, more than ten thousand trees were planted. Maathai's brilliant strategy is simple. She doesn't try to convert villagers to the program; she waits for word of the good work and practical results to spread and, soon enough, the Green Belters are asked to come to another area. In addition to helping to stem the tide of the complete destruction of Kenya's ecosystem, Maathai's Green Belt movement has provided many economic opportunities for Kenya's women.

NATURAL-BORN LEADERS

Zuriel Oduwole is a Nigerian American filmmaker and education advocate. She traveled to Ghana when she was nine to shoot scenes for a documentary she was creating for a national competition, but while she was there, she was stunned to find that so many of the girls there weren't going to school. This inspired her to start an organization called Dream Up, Speak Up, Stand Up, with the purpose of getting more African girls into schools.

Thandiwe Chama is a Zambian educational rights activist who got her start when her school closed due to a lack of teachers. Though she was only eight years old at the time, Chama helped lead her classmates in the search for a new school, and she has persisted in her activism ever since. At sixteen years old, she was awarded the International Children's Peace Prize for her efforts to help more and more children gain access to education. She also advocates for the rights of African individuals living with AIDS and HIV.

In 2014, **Yara Shahidi** landed the role of Zoey Johnson on the TV show *Black-ish*. She has since then used her platform to encourage young people to become more politically involved. She started an organization called We Vote Next (formerly Eighteen x 18) that encourages young adult voter registration and increased voter turnout. She also started a digital meet-up platform for high schoolers to discuss self-improvement and higher education.

At thirteen years old, **Marley Dias** founded a campaign called #1000BlackGirlBooks. Accustomed to only ever reading books about White boys, she initiated this book drive to highlight literature about Black girls. She also has released a book of her very own called *Marley Dias Gets It Done: And So Can You!*

Amariyanna Copeny, or Mari, of Flint, Michigan, wrote a letter to President Obama in early 2016 about the water crisis that was happening in their hometown. Obama replied to her letter and traveled there to help work on a solution. Since then, she has continued to be known as an activist, doing everything she can to help improve life in her community.

Amandla Stenberg's big break was her role as Rue in the film adaptation of *The Hunger Games*. Since then, she has used the internet and her platform to share essays and promote intersectional feminism.

For thirteen-year-old **Zulaikha Patel**, school was a place where she felt marginalized. Pretoria's all-girls high school in South Africa, where Patel attended, had a strict dress-code policy that affected girls of color. Teachers told Patel to "tame" her afro and that her hair was unnatural. This led Patel and other classmates to speak out, and they stood outside the school in protest. By demanding respect, Patel has shown the world that institutional racism still persists, and that students in schools refuse to back down.

Born in Haiti, **Sophia Pierre-Antoine** was inspired by her mother and sister, who both advocated for women's rights. She became involved in the Young Women's Christian Association (YWCA) in Haiti, where she joined in helping young women find a safe haven from abuse. Now, she is on the World YWCA's Global Advisory Council and is the board co-chair for the FRIDA Feminist Fund.

Zianna Oliphant gave an emotional speech at the Charlotte City Council in anger and protest against violence in her community. At just nine years old, she was able to bring attention to police brutality as well as the Black Lives Matter movement on a national level.

In 1963, brave and confident **Audrey Faye Hendricks** left school and joined the Children's Crusade. Held in Birmingham, Alabama, the Children's Crusade was a peaceful demonstration in which thousands of youths contested segregation. Thousands of students, including nine-year-old Hendricks herself, were arrested during the march. She was thrown in the juvenile hall for about a week, making her one of the youngest civil rights demonstrators to be jailed during the movement. The violent actions taken by law enforcement gained international attention on a large scale as photographs taken during the Children's Crusade incensed viewers all over the world.

Nupol Kiazolu is the president of Black Lives Matter Greater New York. At age twelve, outraged by the death of Trayvon Martin, she wore a hoodie to school in protest with the words "Do I look suspicious to you?" written on it. She faced threat of suspension from her school, but refused to take it off, eventually convincing the school principal to let her wear it. Kiazolu aims to inspire Black youth, especially girls, to be active and stand up for themselves. She was also the CEO and founder of Vote2000 at only eighteen years old.

At an early age, **Thandiwe Abdullah** understood that activism was important, which did not make her popular among her peers. Regardless, she cofounded the Black Lives Matter Youth Vanguard, and is also a Black Lives Matter organizer. She showed that passion can come from any age when, at fifteen, she launched the Black Lives Matter in Schools campaign. As a student herself, Abdullah wants to create a safe place for people of color and encourage them to rally against anti-Blackness.

DARNELLA FRAZIER:
Recording History

While taking her nine-year-old niece on what was meant to be a simple trip to Cup Foods, Darnella Frazier witnessed a man, George Floyd, begging for his life as he was forcibly held to the ground with a police officer's knee pressed against his neck. Frazier, who was seventeen at the time, pulled out her cell phone and recorded the incident. The now infamous video went viral and sparked a resurgence in the Black Lives Matter movement, leading to huge protests in cities across the US. Frazier recalls being terrified to get involved and feeling guilty for not doing more, even though her video served as a key piece of evidence in the trial of Derek Chauvin. Frazier was an instrumental figure in this trial, recalling the fear she felt while, along with the other bystanders, she yelled at all officers involved telling them to stop hurting Floyd. Combined with her powerful statements at the trial, Frazier's video evidence was used to convict Derek Chauvin on three counts of murder and manslaughter. Frazier rightfully received the PEN America Award for Courage for her act of bravery, and has been praised by senators, journalists, filmmakers, and President Joe Biden. Frazier is a prime example of not only an awesome girl but a *strong* girl.

IDA B. WELLS:
Journalist for Justice

Ida Bell Wells-Barnett was an African American journalist and advocate of women's rights, including suffrage. Though she was born a slave in 1862 in Holly Springs, Mississippi, six months later the Emancipation Proclamation freed all slaves. Even though they were legally free citizens, her family faced racial prejudice and discrimination while living in Mississippi. Her father helped start Shaw University, and Wells received schooling there, but when she was sixteen, her parents and one of her siblings died of yellow fever. This meant that as the eldest, Wells had to stop going to school and start taking care of her eight sisters and brothers. Since the family direly needed money, Wells ingeniously convinced a county school official that she was eighteen and managed to obtain a job as a teacher. In 1882, she moved to her aunt's in Nashville with several siblings, and at last continued her education at Fisk University.

A direct experience of prejudice in 1884 electrifyingly catalyzed Wells's sense of the need to advocate for justice. While traveling from Memphis to Nashville, she bought a first-class train ticket, but was outraged when the crew told her to move to the car for African Americans. Refusing, Wells was forced off the train; rather than giving in and giving up, she sued the railroad in circuit court and gained a judgment forcing them to pay her $500. Sadly, the State Supreme Court later overturned the decision, but this experience motivated her to write about Southern racial politics and prejudice. Various Black publications published her articles, written under the nom de plume of Iola. Wells later became an owner of two papers, the *Memphis Free Speech and Headlight* and *Free Speech*.

Besides her journalistic and publishing work, she also worked as a teacher at one of Memphis's Black-only public schools. She became a vocal critic of the condition of these segregated schools. This advocacy caused her to be fired from her job in 1891. The next year, three African American store owners clashed with the White owner of a store nearby who felt they were competing too successfully for local business; when the White store owner attacked their store with several allies, the Black store owners ended up shooting several White men while defending their store. The three Black men were taken to jail, but never had their day in court—a lynch mob dragged them out and murdered all three men. Moved to action by this horrible tragedy, Wells started writing about the lynchings of a friend and others, and went on to do in-depth investigative reporting on lynchings in America, risking her life to do so.

While away in New York, Wells was told that her office had been trashed by a mob, and that if she ever came back to Memphis she would be killed. She remained in the North and published an in-depth article on lynching for the *New York Age*, a paper owned by a former slave; she then toured abroad, lecturing on the issue in the hope of enlisting the support of pro-reform White people. When she found out that Black exhibitors were banned at the 1893 World's Columbian Exposition, she published a pamphlet with the support and backing of famed freed slave and abolitionist Frederick Douglass, as well as "A Red Record," a personal report on lynchings in America.

In 1896, Wells founded the National Association of Colored Women, and in 1898 she took her anti-lynching campaign to the White House and led a protest in Washington, DC, to urge President McKinley to act. She was a founding member of the NAACP (National Association for the Advancement of Colored People), but later cut ties with the organization, feeling that it wasn't sufficiently focused on taking action. Wells also worked on behalf of all women and was a part of the National Equal Rights League; she continuously fought for women's suffrage. She even ran for the state senate in 1930, but the next year her health failed, and she died of kidney disease at the age of sixty-eight. Wells's life is a testament to courage in the face of danger.

> **"I felt that one had better die fighting against injustice than to die like a dog or rat in a trap. I had already determined to sell my life as dearly as possible if attacked. I felt if I could take one lyncher with me, this would even up the score a little bit."**

RUTH CHARLOTTE ELLIS:
Oldest Surviving Lesbian

Ruth Charlotte Ellis became widely known as the oldest surviving open lesbian and a queer rights activist. She lived to be 101 years old. She once said, "I was always out of the closet. I didn't have to come out." Ellis was active in the gay rights movement well into her old age. Starting around her seventieth birthday, she became a regular feature of the Michigan Womyn's Festival due to her prominence in the gay community. On her hundredth birthday, a chorus at the San Francisco Dyke March serenaded her with "Happy Birthday to You." Ellis died in 2000, but a center for queer youth, The Ruth Ellis Center, was opened in her honor. It is one of only four agencies in the United States currently serving LGBTQIA+ homeless youth, and has a drop-in center, street outreach program, licensed foster-care home, and a health and wellness center that provides medical and mental healthcare.

MISS MAJOR GRIFFIN-GRACY:
Forty Years of Fighting for Trans Rights

Miss Major Griffin-Gracy is a transgender rights activist who has been fighting for transgender rights for over forty years. She's originally from Chicago but moved to New York City in the 1960s and learned quickly that there was a need for increased safety protections for her and her peers. She helped lead the Stonewall Riots in 1969, and suffered a broken jaw during the police action. She was also part of the rebellion at Attica State Prison where inmates held correctional officers hostage until their demands for better living conditions were discussed. In the 1980s and 1990s, she lived in California and helped her community, which was impacted by the AIDS epidemic. She most recently served as executive director of the Transgender Gender Variant Intersex Justice Project, which helps transgender, gender variant, and intersex people inside and outside of the prison and detention system.

● ● ● ● ●

Black female activists are changing the world we live in one cause at a time. From the green belt of Kenya to the streets of cities all around the globe, these activists are making a difference and putting their bodies behind their beliefs. This is not a new phenomenon: Black women have been protesting for years and years, but their voices are growing louder and more urgent as we face global climate change and the myriad issues plaguing the modern world. Best thing to do is join them.

Chapter 5: SHE-EOs and SHEroes

From the Boardroom to Beyond

Black women have started media companies, clothing lines, and beauty businesses all while balancing their home lives with giving back to the community. They didn't just create businesses, they found solutions to problems with their products. And if they weren't building empires, these women were giving to the community by starting scholarship funds, building schools, or educating the public about problems in society. Media moguls like **Oprah Winfrey** have proven that you don't have to be cold hearted to be a queen. Oprah's school in Africa has educated hundreds of young girls. First Lady **Michelle Obama** set out to get the country moving with her Let's Move! Campaign, and **Karen Arrington** has helped give out $450,000 in scholarships each year as founder of the Miss Black USA pageant.

Madam C.J. Walker became known as the first Black female millionaire in America, but she built her beauty empire on the philosophy of giving back. Her outreach programs helped thousands of young women learn business skills and practical skills like budgeting and finance. This attitude of doing what's right for the community has helped establish Black women among the echelons of top philanthropists.

It's not just adults who are making a difference in the boardroom and on the streets. Young entrepreneur **Asia Newson** provides food and clothing to less-fortunate kids with the proceeds from her candle company (she also buys her own school supplies). Black women learn to give back early, and this early interest in the community carries over, making them into adults who have a broad view of the situation for the less fortunate among us. Some of the women discussed in this chapter also have an eye out for the littlest creatures and on sustaining global health.

After learning about the important role that bees play in the global ecosystem, **Mikaila Ulmer** wanted to protect the honeybee from extinction. A portion of the profits she receives from her honey-sweetened lemonade goes toward ensuring honeybee survival.

Whether they are tycoons or little girls, Black women with an eye for business and philanthropy are making the world a better place, one donation at a time.

ASIA NEWSON:
A Shining Light in the Business World

"Detroit's Youngest Entrepreneur" started her own candle business modeled after her father's sales career. Asia Newson's company blew up, and after several years she is still creating and selling candles. Her business has since grown into Super Business Girl, a workshop-based mentorship program. The company, of which she is cofounder and CEO, gives back to children just like her so that they can learn how to become entrepreneurs too. From the proceeds of the sales, Newson buys her school supplies and purchases food and clothing for less-fortunate kids.

> **"You can't give up because you're a child. And you can't be afraid to fail. That's one thing that I've learned."**

TAKE IT TO THE BANK

Maggie Lena Walker became the first Black American woman to establish and serve as president of a US bank, St. Luke Penny Savings Bank (since 1930, the Consolidated Bank and Trust Company) in Richmond, Virginia.

Kiko Davis is the only Black female owner of an American bank. As trustee to the Donald Davis Living Trust, she acquired a majority stockholder position with First Independence Bank, the tenth-largest Black-owned bank in the United States. As part of its legacy, The Donald Davis Living Trust, named in honor of her husband, also controls several Grammy nomination categories.

MARY ELLEN PLEASANT:
Millionaire Mogul

Mary Ellen Pleasant was arguably the nation's first Black female millionaire. She was a powerful Black woman in Gold Rush-era San Francisco and helped expand the Underground Railroad west to California. Accounts differ on whether she was born into slavery, but by the 1920s she was working in a busy shop in New England. There she met her first husband, James Smith, a contractor and carpenter who left her a large inheritance when he died. She set sail for San Francisco in 1852. The city was booming from the Gold Rush, and some wise investing on Pleasant's part enabled her to buy several boardinghouses and laundries, which were staffed by mostly Black employees. She continued investing in property in San Francisco and nearby Oakland, all the while working as a housekeeper for several prominent White business owners. This position gave her access to free business advice gleaned from eavesdropping on conversations in the merchants' homes. She was a big investor in real estate and mining stock, two booming industries during the Gold Rush. On the 1890 census she declared herself a "capitalist by profession." Pleasant used her wealth to help other Blacks in the San Francisco area. She contributed to the Athenaeum Building, a library and meeting place for Black scholars. She also supported the Black press and the American Methodist Episcopal Zion Church. She was not afraid to speak up when there was injustice, and successfully sued a San Francisco streetcar company when they refused to stop to provide her service even though there was room on the streetcar and she had purchased tickets. After the case, which made it all the way to the California Supreme Court, segregation on streetcars was outlawed in California. When she died, her tombstone was etched at her request with the epigraph, "A friend of John Brown."

MADAM C.J. WALKER:
From Unfortunate to a Fortune

Madam C.J. Walker was an American entrepreneur and one of the first Black American female millionaires. She made her fortune in hair care.

Walker was born Sarah Breedlove in 1867, just outside of Delta, Louisiana. She was the youngest of six children, and the first to be born free after the Emancipation Proclamation. All her brothers and her sister were born into slavery. Her mother died in 1872, and her father died a year later, making her an orphan by the age of seven. She went to live with her sister Louvenia in Vicksburg, Mississippi. As a child, she worked as a domestic servant to help her family make ends meet. The only education she had was three months of literacy training at a church Sunday school.

She married her first husband, Moses McWilliams, when she was fourteen, to get away from her abusive brother-in-law. She and her husband had one daughter. Her husband died in 1887, when she was twenty years old and her daughter was two. In 1888, she moved with her daughter to St. Louis, Missouri, to be close to three of her brothers. At the time, it was a common problem among Black women to have severe dandruff and scalp issues. Walker herself suffered from baldness, probably because of a combination of issues, including a poor diet. Her brothers worked in a barbershop and she started learning about scalp care from them. She went on to work for an entrepreneur named Annie Malone, selling hair care products and eventually developing her own line.

In 1906, she married Charles Joseph Walker and became known as Madam C.J. Walker. That same year, she and her husband began a mail-order service for her products, opened a beauty parlor, and began a training academy to teach beauticians the Walker method. At the height of her career, Walker employed several thousand saleswomen. She had a very active advertising campaign and put her image on all of her products. In addition to her hair care business, Walker taught Black women how to manage their money, build their own businesses, and become financially independent. She was active in several different political and civic organizations and was known for her charity to different causes. When she died in 1919, she was worth between $500,000 and $1 million, easily the wealthiest Black woman in America.

"Don't sit down and wait for the opportunities to come. Get up and make them!"

LARGE AND IN CHARGE

Rosalind Brewer is an American businesswoman, the COO of Starbucks, and the former president and CEO of Sam's Club, a division of Wal-Mart Stores Inc. In a public interview, she spoke about how she chose to go to a historically Black college simply because she could identify with the people and individual professors invested in her like family.

Ursula Burns of Xerox Corporation became the first Black American female CEO of a Fortune 500 company.

Janice Bryant Howroyd is the first Black CEO to build a billion-dollar personnel company. Born in 1952 in Tarboro, North Carolina, Howroyd was one of the first students to

desegregate her previously segregated high school. She worked as a temporary secretary for her brother-in-law at *Billboard* magazine. While there, Howroyd learned different decision-making strategies and was introduced to many luminaries in the business world. She started ActOne Group, Inc. with little more than $1,000 and industry knowledge. In the years since she opened her business, she has seen it grow into a billion-dollar personnel company that provides employment, workforce management, and procurement solutions to Fortune 500 organizations, local and mid-market companies, and government agencies.

Sheila Johnson is an American businesswoman, cofounder of BET, and CEO of Salamander Hotels and Resorts. She saw the importance of ownership, which led her to be the first African American woman to own over three professional sports franchises.

ELIZABETH HOBBS KECKLEY:
Dressmaker to the Lincolns

Elizabeth Hobbs Keckley was a former slave who became a successful seamstress, author, and civil rights activist in Washington, DC. She was first lady Mary Todd Lincoln's personal dressmaker. Keckley's father was also her owner, Armistead Burwell. Keckley's mother was a light-skinned house slave, and Elizabeth learned to sew at an early age from working in the house with her. Keckley was primarily a nursemaid to the Burwell children, and was severely beaten if she failed in her duties. Her mother was permitted to marry another slave at a neighboring house, George Hobbs, who was sold off when Keckley was young. He corresponded with her mother for many years, which was rare at the time because slaves were not allowed to read and write.

In 1855, she bought her freedom and that of her son for $1,200, for which she took out on loan from some of her patrons. After she paid off her debt, she moved to Baltimore, Maryland, where she tried to set up a business teaching young Black women to sew, but was unsuccessful. She then moved to Washington, DC, where she found more success in business and began to take dress orders from prominent White women in the capital, including Varina Davis, wife of Jefferson Davis. She employed twenty seamstresses at her business and was known for fitting garments for her patrons that complimented their figures. She met Mary Todd Lincoln on President Lincoln's Inauguration Day in 1861, and was hired the next day to become Mrs. Lincoln's personal dresser.

Keckley became an intimate part of the Lincoln White House, and she was considered to be Mrs. Lincoln's best friend. She was often called upon to style President Lincoln's unruly hair. When the Lincoln's son Willie died, it was Keckley who Mrs. Lincoln called to help console her. She was also called upon to console Mrs. Lincoln after her husband was assassinated. When Mrs. Lincoln went into debt after her husband's death, she called upon Keckley to help her sell off some of her wardrobe to meet her debts. The result was a disastrous scandal for Mrs. Lincoln, who was seen as gauche for trying to sell off her old clothes. In 1868, Keckley published a memoir, *Behind the Scenes or Thirty Years a Slave, and Four Years in the White House*. It did not go over well with the public, who were scandalized that Keckley told of so many of the Lincoln's private moments. But the memoir was not just an account of her time at the White House, it was also a narrative of her path to freedom, and of the many years of hard work she put into dressing the elite of Washington.

MAYA PENN:
Eco-Friendly Fashionista

Maya Penn is a young entrepreneur who was born and raised in Atlanta. In 2008, at the age of eight, she started Maya's Ideas, her own eco-friendly fashion house. She partners with major brands to help them address sustainability and find ways to make fashion friendlier for the environment, promoting the development of eco-consciousness in the industry. She has also done three TED talks that have gone viral, and was chosen as Oprah's youngest SuperSoul100 entrepreneur.

"Be creative, be curious, and watch as your awesomeness is unleashed."

EUNICE W. JOHNSON:
Media Giant

Eunice W. Johnson was creator of Fashion Fair Cosmetics and co-creator of the *Negro Digest, Ebony,* and *Jet* magazines. She helped bring Black representation to mainstream America at a time when Black people were sorely under-represented in the media. She was born in 1916 in Selma, Alabama. Her mother was a high school principal and her father was a physician. She studied sociology at Talladega University. In 1940, while attending a master's degree program at Loyola University, she met her future husband, John H. Johnson. They married in 1941 after she received her master's degree. In 1942, Johnson and her husband began publication of the *Negro Digest,* which was designed to emulate *Reader's Digest.* The magazine grew in popularity so quickly that they were inspired to create *Ebony* magazine, a monthly publication, and then *Jet* magazine, its weekly sister publication. Johnson suggested the name of the dark wood for *Ebony.* By the time of her death, *Ebony's* circulation had reached 1.25 million readers, and *Jet* was reaching 900,000. The magazines brought Black interests into the homes of many Black families, and were influential in a number of ways. They both printed stories dedicated to Black interests, hired Black writers, and covered issues like the Civil Rights Movement for a Black audience. This was at a time when there were few publications solely devoted to a Black audience. Starting in 1958, Johnson ran the Ebony Fashion Tour (which later became Ebony Fashion Fair), an international tour that was started to aid a hospital in New Orleans. The fashion tour featured designs by Black designers and Black models. In its fifty years of existence, the tour reached over five hundred locations across the United States and Caribbean. Johnson also launched Fashion Fair Cosmetics, a line of makeup designed specifically for darker skin tones. The business took off and helped bring makeup to millions of Black women who were not represented by the pale palettes associated with popular cosmetics. Eunice Johnson died in 2010 at the age of ninety-three. The magazines she spearheaded are still published today.

• • • • •

Younger Black women are making strides in the business world too. The scope of their contributions to society and the economy is often overlooked. Often these young SHE-EOs pair their business model with an impetus to solve a global problem, making them not just entrepreneurs but philanthropists as well.

CaShawn Thompson, creator of #BlackGirlMagic, was able to build this brand at the age of forty, without a degree, without a husband, and without checking all of the world's boxes of success. Black Girl Magic has been endorsed by

Regina King and Beyonce, but the heart behind #BGM is its encouragement of beauty and strength within the most average of Black girls. Black Girl Magic is for all the Black and Brown girls.

MIKAILA ULMER:
Queen Bee

At four years old, Mikaila Ulmer learned about bees' importance in the environment and decided that she wanted to do something to protect them. She entered a local business competition for children in the area with her family's homemade lemonade recipe, sweetening the lemonade with locally produced honey. She donated a portion of sales toward conservation organizations working to prevent the extinction of honeybees. She has sold her Me & the Bees lemonade at events, and went on *Shark Tank* to grow the business. She was even able to secure a partnership with Whole Foods!

"Don't be discouraged by life's little stings, get back up and spread your wings!"

ANNIE TURNBO MALONE:
A Generous Entrepreneur

Annie Turnbo Malone was an inventor, philanthropist, and businesswoman. She was one of the first Black women to become a self-made millionaire. She was born in 1869 in Illinois, the tenth of eleven children, and was orphaned at an early age. An older sister raised her. She attended high school in Peoria, Illinois, where she excelled in chemistry, but had to withdraw from classes due to frequent illnesses. Malone took an interest in hair care and would often style her sister's hair. Sometime around 1900, she invented a product that would straighten Black hair without damaging it, unlike most of the products at the time. She then developed an entire line of hair and beauty products for Black women, but needed a larger market than the one she found in Illinois. She moved to St. Louis, Missouri, in 1902. St. Louis was booming from the World's Fair, and Malone and her employees began going door to door to sell their products, because as Black women they were denied regular distribution channels. After a positive response at the World's Fair, Malone and her company went national, selling her products all across the United States. She married a school principal in 1914, and by the end of World War I, she was a millionaire. Malone was very generous with her money and donated to several organizations, including the St. Louis Colored Orphans Home. She established Poro College in St. Louis in 1918. Her wealth was threatened when her husband filed for divorce and demanded half her business, but she settled with him for $200,000 and moved to Chicago for a fresh start. Money troubles continued to follow Malone: her business was hit hard by the 1929 stock market crash, but she remained in business and by the mid-1950s, had opened thirty-two branches of the Poro School across the United States. She continued to be a philanthropist until her death in 1957.

• • • • •

Sometimes the path to philanthropy is one that is forged with intention, but sometimes it is forged by sheer luck and chance. **Mary J. Blige**, American singer-songwriter, actress, and philanthropist, dropped out of high school when a karaoke booth recording of her singing "Caught Up in the Rapture" reached Uptown Records. She went on to win nine Grammy awards. Blige gives back because it's the right thing to do, but who knows where she would have ended up had the karaoke recording not reached Uptown Records. In the next section we'll explore the giving nature of some Black women in order to gain an understanding of what causes they support and why.

Black women give back. Perhaps it is because Black businesswomen come from a history of oppression and hardship that they tend to be charitable with their profits. Far from the model of the cold-hearted capitalist the world has come to expect, many Black businesswomen use their wealth and power to contribute to society, and make the world an easier place in which to live for the unfortunate and under-served. These next titans sank their fortunes into endeavors for the less fortunate.

OPRAH WINFREY:
The Queen of the Talk Show

Although most people think of *The Oprah Winfrey Show*
when they think of Oprah, besides ruling the media world as a
television and talk show host, her curriculum vitae also includes
being an actress, producer, magazine publisher, entrepreneur,
CEO, and philanthropist. None of this was handed to her—she
was born to a teenage mother on a farm in Mississippi in 1954,
and her unmarried parents soon separated and left her there
in her grandmother's care. She was exceptionally bright; her
grandmother taught her to read at the tender age of two and
a half, and she was skipped through kindergarten and second
grade. At age six, Winfrey was sent to live with her mother and
three half-siblings in a very rough Milwaukee ghetto. She has
said that she was molested as a child starting at age nine, and
in her early teens by men her family trusted.

At twelve, she was again uprooted and sent to live with her
father, a barber, in Nashville. This, however, was a relatively
positive time for the young Winfrey, who started being called
on to make speeches at churches and social gatherings. After
being paid $500 for a speech on one occasion, she knew she
wanted to be "paid to talk." She was further bounced back
and forth between both her parents' homes, compounding
the trauma of the abuse she had suffered. Her mother worked
long and variable hours and was not around much of the time.
At fourteen, Winfrey became pregnant with a son; he did not
survive early infancy. After some years of acting out, including
running away once, she was sent to her father, to stay this
time. She credits her father with saving her with his strictness

and devotion, his rules, guidance, structure, and books. It was mandatory that she write a book report every week, and she went without dinner unless she learned five new vocabulary words every day.

Things completely turned around for Winfrey. She did well in school and then managed to land a job in radio while still in high school. After winning an oratory contest, she was able to study communication on a scholarship at Tennessee State University, a historically Black college. She was a co-anchor of the local evening news at age nineteen, and before long her emotional verve when ad-libbing took her into the world of Baltimore's daytime talk shows. After seven years on *Baltimore Is Talking*, she had better local ratings than those of famed national talk show host Phil Donahue. She took a local Chicago talk show from third place to first, and was then on her way with the launch of her own production company. In 1985, a year after taking on *A.M. Chicago*, producer Quincy Jones spotted her on air and decided to cast her in a film he was planning based on Alice Walker's novel *The Color Purple*. Her acting in this extremely well-received film had a meteoric effect on the popularity of her talk show, which was by now *The Oprah Winfrey Show*, and the show gained wide syndication. She had taken a local show and changed its focus from traditional women's concerns and tabloid fodder to issues including cancer, charity work, substance abuse, self-improvement, geopolitics, literature, and spirituality.

Winfrey launched *O: The Oprah Magazine* in 2000; it continues to be popular. She has spearheaded other publications as well, from four years of *O At Home* magazine to coauthoring five books. In 2008, she created a new channel called OWN:

Oprah Winfrey Network, and put her self-branded talk show to bed. She has earned the sobriquet of "Queen of All Media," and is counted the richest African American and the most pre-eminent Black philanthropist in American history. She is at present North America's first and only Black multi-billionaire, and is considered to be one of the most influential women in the world, despite the many setbacks and hardships she endured in early life. She has been awarded honorary doctorates from Duke and Harvard universities, and in 2013, she received the Presidential Medal of Freedom from President Barack Obama.

MICHELLE OBAMA:
Fearless FLOTUS

Michelle Obama not only served as the forty-fourth first lady of the United States of America but is also a lawyer, writer, and the founder of Let's Move!, an initiative geared toward the prevention of child obesity, as well as an advocate of civil rights for women and LGBT people. Michelle Robinson was born in Chicago in 1964. In 1985 she graduated from Princeton, and in 1988 she completed a law degree at the prestigious Harvard Law School, after which she worked at Sidley Austin, a Chicago corporate law firm of high repute. Though Sidley didn't usually take on first-year law students as associates, in 1989 they asked her to mentor a summer associate named Barack Obama. When he finished his term as an associate and returned to Harvard, their relationship continued long distance, and in 1992 they married. At the same time, she was evaluating in those years whether a career in corporate law was really what she wanted. Corporate law, while lucrative, was not what she'd intended when she started college. She lost her father to kidney complications in 1991, which furthered her process of reflection; she was later quoted by the *New York Times* as saying, "I wanted to have a career motivated by passion and not just money." She left Sidley Austin and went to work for Chicago, first for the mayor and then providing her expertise to Valerie Jarrett, the head of the Planning and Development Department. In that position, she was working to create jobs and bring new life to Chicago's neighborhoods, and after this turning point she never looked back.

After spending a few years working in hospital administration for the University of Chicago, Michelle Obama became first lady of the United States when her husband won the presidential election of 2008. In this role, she advocated for military families, working women balancing their family with their career, and arts and arts education. She also supported LGBTQIA+ civil rights, working with her husband for the passage of the Employment Non-Discrimination Act and the repeal of Don't Ask Don't Tell. In 2010, she began to take steps to create a healthier lifestyle for the youth of America with the Let's Move campaign to prevent child obesity. These are just a few of many of her accomplishments as the first African American first lady in the White House. Since leaving the White House, she has continued her advocacy work and even written a memoir.

"There are still many causes worth sacrificing for, so much history yet to be made."

BEAUTY WITH A HEART

Liya Kebede was born in 1978 in Addis Ababa, Ethiopia. A film director noticed her distinctive features while she was still a schoolgirl attending Lycée Guebre-Mariam. Impressed by her unique look, the film director immediately recommended her to a French modeling agency. This opened up many opportunities for Kebede, and at the age of eighteen she moved to France to model for a Parisian agency before later relocating to New York City. Things started to really take off for her when she was offered an exclusive contract by designer Tom Ford for his fashion show for the Gucci Fall/ Winter 2000 line, which was also the year she married Kassy Kebede. The cover of *Vogue France* followed: the entire issue was dedicated to her. Kebedehas modeled for designers including Dolce & Gabbana, Louis Vuitton, Yves Saint Laurent, Emanuel Ungaro, Tommy Hilfiger, Shiatzy Chen, and Escada. But Liya Kebede is more than just another pretty face. She was selected to be the WHO's goodwill ambassador for maternal, newborn, and child health in 2005, and soon started the Liya Kebede Foundation, which works for the health of mothers and infants and to prevent child mortality in her native Ethiopia and other African countries. The foundation has gone on to train health workers who have assisted in more than ten thousand births, as well as conducting global maternal health awareness campaigns that have reached millions. It also funds advocacy and supports low-cost technologies, training and medical programs, and community-based education. Kebede has also participated in Champions for an AIDS-Free Generation, a group of African heads of state and other leaders working to end the HIV epidemic. She has used her fame to help people look at the bigger picture, and brought attention to the health of mothers and their children.

Beauty mogul **Lisa Price** is the founder and CEO of Carol's Daughter, one of the first Black-owned businesses with a flagship store. She was born in 1962 in Brooklyn, New York. As a child, her grandmother made soap in the family's brownstone in Brooklyn. Price can still remember the smell. That childhood memory inspired her to create her own product line, which she began producing from her home in 1993. Soon her customer base began expanding along with her product line, which has grown to more than three hundred products for face, hair, body, and home. Her clientele includes Will Smith, Jada Pinkett-Smith, Oprah Winfrey, Halle Berry, and Chaka Khan. In 2002, Carol's Daughter grossed more than $2.25 million in sales. In 2004, she published her memoir, *Success Never Smelled So Sweet: How I Followed My Nose and Found My Passion*. In 2005, a group of investors helped her open her flagship store in Harlem. Carol's Daughter gives back to the community with the proceeds of their sales. Benefactors include the Arthur Ashe Foundation, Hale House, and the September 11 Fund. Price also speaks at colleges and universities where she encourages others to take up entrepreneurship.

Rihanna is a Barbadian singer, songwriter, actress, businesswoman, and philanthropist. She successfully launched her own cosmetic line, Fenty Beauty, featuring affordable makeup aimed at solving the diversity issues in the skincare world.

KAREN ARRINGTON:
More than Just a Pretty Face

Karen Arrington is the founder of the Miss Black USA Pageant. More than a pageant, it's a movement—celebrating the talents and achievements of today's Black women and awarding over $450,000 in college scholarships each year. Since founding the pageant in 1986, Arrington has mentored over a thousand young women, helping them get into top medical schools, land major modeling and recording contracts, secure life-changing grants and sponsorship deals, and more. In addition to running the pageant, Arrington is a philanthropist and humanitarian whose work has touched millions of lives. She's the cofounder of Diabetes Awareness Day in West Africa and was named a goodwill ambassador to the Gambia and to the Republic of Sierra Leone. She has received numerous awards, including leadership awards from the Lifetime Network and Jones New York, the Trailblazer's Award by Zeta Phi Sorority (the highest award that is bestowed by this sorority, which has over 21,000 members), and Maryland Black Mayors Honors for commitment and dedication to the community, and she was a *Woman's Day* magazine Red Dress Honoree along with CNN's Sanjay Gupta and Olympic gold medalist Dana Vollmer. Arrington has been interviewed in places like the *Washington Post*, *Woman's Day*, *Jet*, and on BET.

• • • • •

By giving back, these entrepreneurs are also investing in the future and ensuring that others have a hand-up in life. They could easily pocket their earnings, but they choose to get involved with their communities and make sure the future is brighter for others who are less fortunate than they are. The ties that Black women have with their communities are deep, meaningful, and lasting, and by giving back to the community, the world becomes a little more cozy and welcoming for everyone.

Chapter 6: Mighty in the Classroom, the Military, & the Church

Black Women Leading the Way

In the classroom, in military service, and in the church, Black women have been not only the glue that holds the community together but also served as leaders and role models to younger generations of women. And these weren't just young women. **Nana Yaa Asantewa** was fifty when she led a rebellion against the British in Ghana, proving it is never too late in life to make a difference. These women led with elegance and poise while being burdened with making the hardest decisions one could ever have to make; but by doing so, they made history and proved that women do, in fact, rule.

Black women have had to balance the demands of the spotlight with the demands of family life as well. After her husband Malcolm X's assassination, **Betty X** balanced a rich public-speaking life with the demands of a doctoral program, all while raising six daughters on her own.

Black women have also tended to the world's children. Pastor **Esther Ibanga** of Nigeria has been instrumental in the Bring Back Our Girls campaign to free 276 schoolgirls who had been kidnapped by Boko Haram terrorists.

Black women are known for their compassion and for picking up the pieces when the world is falling apart. **Katy Ferguson** ministered to orphans on the streets of New York and brought them inside for Sunday school, and she is just one example of the powerful, dedicated Black women in military service, in the classroom, or in church who embody the inner strength and determination needed to make a difference in the lives of those around them, and in some cases, on a global scale.

For many years, education was out of reach for Black women. Not allowed to read nor write under discriminatory laws during slavery, Black women learned to rely on an oral tradition of passing down history and folklore. Once the ban on reading and writing was lifted and Black women began to gain educations there was no stopping them, and they rose through the class ranks to join the upper tier of graduates. Historically Black colleges and universities helped them in their quest for knowledge. Established specifically to educate freed Black people after the Civil War, Black colleges and universities are still thriving across

America, and offer a safe place in which students can study their subjects with a culturally relevant group of peers.

MARY MCLEOD BETHUNE:
A Dollar and a Dream

In 1904, Mary McLeod Bethune started a school with $1.50 and dreams on the grounds of a former dump. "I haunted the city dump retrieving discarded linen and kitchenware, cracked dishes, broken chairs, pieces of old lumber," she remembered later. The humble beginning has now blossomed into Bethune-Cookman University in Daytona, Florida.

She wasn't daunted by the idea of all the hard work it would take to make her dreams come true; she was used to picking 250 pounds of cotton a day and pulling the plow when the family mule died. The fifteenth of seventeen children born to former slaves, Bethune was brought up as a strict Methodist to believe in the sweat of the brow and faith in God. At the age of twelve, she was given a scholarship by the Quakers to be educated at an integrated school in North Carolina, later going on to the Moody Bible Institute of Chicago. From these experiences she developed a profound respect for education, particularly for its value in helping her people rise from poverty.

Bethune's school succeeded through her combination of penny-pinching abilities and excellent fundraising skills (she even got J.D. Rockefeller to contribute). She trained the students to pick elderberries to make into ink, used burned wood for chalk, and bartered free tuition for food for her students. Soon she added an infirmary on the site when she realized Black people couldn't get medical treatment within 200 miles of that part of the Atlantic Coast; eventually this grew into a training hospital for doctors and nurses. By 1922, the school boasted three hundred students, and Bethune stayed on as president of the college until 1942.

She had a strong commitment to African Americans, particularly women. While running the school, she led a campaign to register Black women voters, despite threats from the KKK. Her civil rights activism and humanitarianism brought her into contact with many people, including Eleanor Roosevelt, with whom she became good friends. Bethune ended up serving people in many leadership roles, including as the founder and president of the National Council of Negro Women, the leading member of the "Black Cabinet," who were advisors to FDR on African American needs and interests, and as the director of the Office of Minority Affairs of the National Youth Administration. When she was seventy-seven, concerned over the inability of Black people to get life insurance, she started the Central Life Insurance Company, becoming the only woman president of a national life insurance company in the entire United States.

For these and other accomplishments, Mary McLeod Bethune was regarded as the most influential Black woman in America until her death in 1955. Her rise from poverty to national leadership is sheer SHEroism.

"I leave you. I leave you hope...I leave you racial dignity."

FIRSTS IN EDUCATION

The women below were pioneers in education, gaining diplomas and achieving positions in education that were unheard of just years before they met their achievements. Black women are still under-represented in education today. There's a good chance that a student can attend a K–12 school without ever having a Black teacher, and when they are hired, Black women teachers make less money than their White counterparts, and often serve in poorer school districts where the resources are far sparser than at schools in wealthier neighborhoods.

Sarah Jane Woodson Early became America's first Black female college professor. She joined the Wilberforce College faculty in 1858.

Mary Jane Patterson made history when she graduated in 1862 from Oberlin College with a Bachelor of Arts degree, becoming the first Black American woman to earn a degree from that school.

Fanny Jackson Coppin became the first Black American female school principal at the Institute for Colored Youth.

Hortense Parker is the first-known Black American woman to graduate from one of the Seven Sisters colleges. She earned her degree at Mount Holyoke Seminary, now Mount Holyoke College.

Sadie Tanner Mossell Alexander was the first Black American woman to earn a PhD in economics, in 1921, and the first woman to earn a law degree, in 1927. She earned both of her degrees at the University of Pennsylvania.

Elizabeth Duncan Koontz was the first Black American woman elected president of the National Education Association, in 1968.

Shirley Ann Jackson was the first Black American woman university president in the United States. She rose to the president's office at Rensselaer Polytechnic Institute in Troy, New York.

Marva Collins, American educator, opened her own school in her own home due to her frustrations with the Chicago school system. After that first year, all the students scored five grades higher than normal. She went on to receive more than forty honorary degrees, and her school remained open for over thirty years.

SEPTIMA POINSETTE CLARK:
Living Legacy

Septima Poinsette Clark was an educator and civil rights activist. She was born in Charleston, South Carolina, in 1898. Her father had been born into slavery, and her mother, while born in Charleston, was raised in Haiti. Her mother returned to the United States and worked as a launderer, and had very strict rules in the household; Clark was only allowed to play with other children one day a week. She attended school at a neighbor's house and learned to read and write there. In exchange for her tuition, Clark watched the woman's children. There was no high school in Charleston at the time for Black students, but a Black middle school opened up. She took a test in the sixth grade and was able to go on to the ninth grade at the Avery Normal Institute, a private school for Black students. She worked to earn the money for her tuition there.

After high school, Clark qualified to work as a teacher, but she wasn't able to teach in Charleston because she was Black, so she taught on Johns Island in South Carolina instead. In 1919, she took a job teaching at the Avery Normal Institute and joined the NAACP, where she helped gather signatures for a petition to have Charleston begin hiring Black teachers. The petition was a success. She later moved to Columbia, South Carolina, where she joined the local chapter of the NAACP and fought for equal pay for Black teachers. The NAACP was successful, and Clark's salary tripled after the ruling! She moved back to Charleston for a teaching position in 1947, but South Carolina had made it illegal for public employees to join civil rights organizations. Clark refused to give up her NAACP membership and lost her job.

She was hired by Highlander Folk School in Tennessee. The school supported integration and civil rights. Clark began directing the Citizenship School program, which helped teach basic math and literacy skills to people in the community. This was important because at the time many places in the South required literacy tests for people to vote. In 1961, when the Southern Christian Leadership Conference (SCLC) took over the program, she joined the SCLC as its director of education and teaching. She helped create more than eight hundred citizenship schools. Clark wrote two memoirs *Echo in My Soul* and *Ready from Within: Septima Clark and Civil Rights*. Her second memoir won an American Book Award. In 1979, President Jimmy Carter awarded her with a Living Legacy Award, and in 1982 she received the Order of the Palmetto, South Carolina's highest civilian award. Septima Clark died in 1987.

VIVIAN E.J. COOK:
Principal Activist

Vivian E.J. Cook was an educator and activist. She was born in Collierville, Tennessee, in 1889. Her parents were both born into slavery. Cook's mother Caroline became the first Black school teacher in Fayette County, Tennessee, and she ensured that her children received educations. Cook graduated from Howard University in 1912. After graduating from Howard, she taught at the Tuskegee Institute, in Cincinnati, Ohio, and in St.

Louis, Missouri, at Sumner High School. She graduated from Columbia University in 1917 with a master's degree. In 1918, she married and moved to Baltimore, Maryland, where she worked in the school district as a teacher, vice principal, and principal of several schools in the city. She was the first Black woman to hold an administrative position at a secondary school in Baltimore. Cook was active in several social and advocacy groups, including the National Association of College Women. In 1938, she served on the African American subcommittee of the Baltimore Museum of Art's Committee of the City. While serving on that committee, Cook suggested that there be an educational portion to the 1939 exhibition "Contemporary Negro Art." She also collaborated on other projects highlighting African American art for the Baltimore Museum of Art, and helped acquire several paintings for the museum. Vivian Cook died in 1977.

DR. ANNA JULIA HAYWOOD COOPER:
A Voice from the South

Dr. Anna Julia Haywood Cooper was a writer, intellectual, teacher, and activist. She championed education for Black scholars. She was born into bondage in 1858, the daughter of a slave and her owner. In 1867, two years after the end of the Civil War, she began her education at St. Augustine's Normal School and Collegiate Institute, a coed facility that was opened to educate former slaves. There, she earned the equivalent of a high school diploma. She married a theology professor from St. Augustine's in 1877, but when her husband died two years later, she decided to pursue a college education. She earned a BA and an MA from Oberlin College in Ohio, then went to work teaching at Wilberforce University and St. Augustine's before moving to Washington, DC, to teach at Washington Colored High School.

In 1892, she published her first book, *A Voice from the South by a Black Woman of the South*, which called for equal education for women and argued that education for Black Americans would uplift the entire Black race. The book gained a lot of publicity, and Cooper went on a speaking tour to promote the book of essays. In 1902, she began a controversial tenure as principal of M Street High School in Washington, DC, but resigned after the school board took issue with her policy of preparing Black students for college. During her years teaching, she also helped found several civic organizations, including the Colored Women's League in 1892. She was part of the executive committee at the first Pan African Conference in 1900, and when the YMCA and YWCA would not allow Black people to join, she created "colored" branches to help support Black Americans moving to Washington, DC, from the South.

Cooper returned to graduate school at Columbia University in 1911, but her graduate studies were interrupted by the death of her brother, who had five young grandchildren that needed to be supported. She helped raise them, and then returned to college at the University of Paris in 1924, at the age of sixty-six. In 1925, she became the fourth Black woman to earn a PhD in philosophy. She continued teaching until 1930, when she retired in order to assume the role of president of Frelinghuysen University, a school for Black adults. She assumed the position of registrar of the school when it was reorganized into the Frelinghuysen Group of Schools for Colored People, and remained in that position until the school closed in 1950.

BETTY X:
Activist Scholar

Betty Shabazz, also known as Betty X, was an educator and civil rights leader. She was married to Malcolm X. Betty grew up in Detroit, Michigan. Her foster family did not discuss race relations with her, and as a result of this sheltered upbringing, she was unprepared for the hardships of racism when she moved to Alabama to study at the famed Tuskegee Institute. There she experienced the harsh reality of racism. Unwilling to allow herself to be treated as a second-class citizen, Betty moved to New York City, where she studied nursing. She met Malcolm X at a Nation of Islam dinner, which led to a courtship, and they were married in 1958. After Malcolm X's assassination in 1965, Betty was tasked with raising her six daughters on her own. She was able to survive thanks to royalties from Alex Haley's book *The Autobiography of Malcolm X*, but also returned to school and pursued a doctorate in higher education and curriculum development. She also began to speak nationwide at colleges and universities about civil rights, and began teaching at Medgar Evers College.

Betty was active in the civil rights movement her entire life, and was prominent in the NAACP and Urban League. She befriended Myrlie Evers-Williams and Coretta Scott King (the widows of Medgar Evers and Dr. Martin Luther King Jr., respectively), with whom she shared the common experience of losing their husbands to violence. Betty died after sustaining severe burns in a house fire in 1997.

DIANE NASH:
Freedom Rider

Diane Nash is a civil rights activist and was a leader and strategist of the student wing of the civil rights movement. She cofounded the Student Nonviolent Coordinating Committee and was instrumental in many of the student-led civil rights protests of the era. Nash was born in Chicago, Illinois, and grew up in a Catholic neighborhood. After graduating from high school, she attended Howard University before transferring to Fisk University in Nashville, Tennessee. In Nashville, Nash experienced Southern-style racial segregation for the first time in her life. She took part in the 1959 lunch counter sit-ins in Nashville that led Tennessee to become the first Southern state to desegregate its lunch counters. In 1960, she helped organize the Student Nonviolent Coordinating Committee, which would become a major force in the civil rights era. In 1961, she helped coordinate and participated in the Freedom Rides across the Deep South. Later that year, she became a full-time instructor, strategist, and organizer for the

Southern Christian Leadership Council (SCLC) which was
led by Dr. Martin Luther King Jr. She married and moved
to Mississippi. There she helped organize voter registration
drives and desegregation campaigns in the schools for
the SCLC. She was arrested dozens of times for her actions
in protests, and in 1965, she received the Rosa Parks
Award from Dr. Martin Luther King Jr. In 1966, she joined
the Vietnam Peace Movement. In the 1980s, she fought
for women's rights. Nash continues to be an outspoken
advocate for change even now.

NANNIE HELEN BURROUGHS:
The Practical Prophet

NAACP pioneer William Picken described Nannie Burroughs
this way: "No other person in America has so large a hold
on the loyalty and esteem of the colored masses as Nannie
H. Burroughs. She is regarded all over the broad land as
combination of brains, courage, and incorruptibleness."
Born in the Gilded Age in 1879, Nannie Burroughs was
fortunate to be born into a family of ex-slaves who were
able to establish a comfortable existence in Virginia,
affording young Burroughs a good education. She applied
for a job as a domestic science teacher and wasn't
hired because she was "too dark." Later, she was turned
down for a job as a government clerk because she was a
Black woman.

Burroughs began dreaming of a way to prepare Black
women for careers that freed them from the traps of

gender and bias. She worked for the national Baptist alliance for fifty years, starting as a bookkeeper and secretary. In her spare time, she organized the Women's Industrial Club, providing practical clerical courses for women. Through the school she founded in 1909, the National Training School for Women and Girls, she educated thousands of Black American women as well as Haitians, Puerto Ricans, and South Africans, to send them into the world with the tools for successful careers. Her program emphasized what she called the three Bs: the Bible, the Bath, and the Broom, representing "clean lives, clean bodies, and clean homes."

An advocate of racial self-help, Burroughs worked all her life to provide a solid foundation for poor Black women so they could work and gain independence and equality. She practiced what she preached. At one point she wrote to John D. Rockefeller for a donation to her cause. He sent her one dollar with a note asking what a businesswoman like her would do with the money. She purchased a dollar's worth of peanuts and sent them to him with a note asking him to

autograph each one and return them to her. She would
then sell each one for a dollar.

She founded The Harriet Beecher Stowe Society as a
vehicle for literary expression, and was also active in the
anti-lynching campaigns. She gave Sojourner Truth a run
for her money with dramatic speeches and stirring lectures
such as a headline-making speech in 1932: "Chloroform
your Uncle Toms! What must the Negro do to be saved?
The Negro must unload the leeches and parasitic leaders
who are absolutely eating the life out of the struggling,
frightened mass of people."

One of her students once said that Burroughs considered
"everybody God's nugget." Her pragmatic "grab your
own bootstraps" approach to racial equality offered that
chance to everyone who came into her purview.

● ● ● ● ●

These next Black women were warriors who sometimes
literally fought for justice and equality in the military and
in government positions. As soon as they were given the
right to vote, Black American women have taken on civic
leadership roles in their communities and in state-wide and
national positions of power. Their unique perspective on
what their communities need means that often times Black
women are able to improve their neighborhoods in ways
that other candidates might overlook. The problems within
Black communities are complicated by a lack of investment
in infrastructure and by urban blight. Black women see these

problems and work toward solutions that will benefit their entire community.

YVONNE BRATHWAITE BURKE:
Political Standout

Yvonne Burke was the first Black woman elected to the US House of Representatives from California, serving from 1973–1978. The daughter of a janitor and a real estate agent, the Los Angeles native was noted as exceptionally bright by her teachers and was sent to a model UCLA college prep school. The only African American student at the school, Burke was treated viciously by the other students, but didn't let that stop her from turning in a stellar performance. Everywhere she went, she encountered more bigotry, including the women's law sorority she was turned down by, compelling her to form an alternative women's law sorority with two Jewish law students. Starting with her election in 1972, Burke's career in Congress was equally outstanding, and she was unfailingly supportive of the causes of desegregation, equal employment, and better housing. In 1978, she chose to run for California State attorney general rather than seek reelection. She currently practices law in Los Angeles. Burke is a visionary with the smarts and dignity to rise above the hatred she has personally experienced just for being Black, saying, "It's just a matter of time until we have a black governor and, yes, a black president." With the election of Barack Obama, she was proven right.

NANA YAA ASANTEWAA:
Ghanain Warrior

Nana Yaa Asantewaa was born in 1863 and went on to become the national SHEro of Ghana, known as the Queen Mother. When British colonists stole Ghana's sacred treasure, Asantewaa (at the age of fifty) led an uprising to take back the Golden Stool. She and her army of women were defeated, but her valor and that of her women warriors was legendary. She died in prison at seventy after being a captive exile for twenty years.

ALICE DUNNIGAN:
Hard-Won Credentials

Alice Dunnigan was the first Black female reporter to receive White House press credentials. In 1947, she was the first Black female correspondent to travel with a sitting president when she joined President Harry S. Truman on his campaign tour.

● ● ● ● ●

These next women were the first in their fields. Some excelled in military posts, others served in government positions. Whatever role they took, each of these awe-inspiring ladies was a pioneer in a field dominated by White men, with little historical precedent for their success.

- **Patricia Roberts Harris** was the first Black American woman to hold two cabinet positions. She was secretary of the Department of Housing and Urban Development and secretary of health, education, and welfare during the Carter administration. Harris was also the first Black woman to hold an ambassadorship. She was ambassador to Luxembourg during the Johnson Administration.

- **Barbara Jordan** was the first woman of any color to deliver a keynote address at a Democratic national convention. She was also the first Black person of any gender to be elected to the Texas Senate after Reconstruction, and the first Southern Black person of any gender to be elected to the US House of Representatives.

- **Azie Taylor Morton** was the first Black woman to sign US currency. She was the thirty-sixth treasurer of the United States and remains the only Black woman to have held that post.

- **Amalya Lyle Kearse** was the first woman appointed to the US Court of Appeals and the second Black person of either gender (after Thurgood Marshall). She was named to the Second Circuit in 1979. She is also a world-class bridge player.

- **Constance Baker Motley** was the first Black woman to hold a federal judicial post. She was appointed a US District Court judge on August 30, 1966. She also became the first Black woman to argue a case before the US Supreme Court when she successfully argued *Meredith v Fair* in 1962, which won James Meredith the right to attend the segregated University of Mississippi.

- **Bessie Stringfield** became the first Black woman to ride a motorcycle alone across the lower connected forty-eight states. She took this trip alone eight times, and served as the only Black civilian female motorcycle courier for the US Army during World War II.

- **Vernice Armour**, USMC captain, was the first Black American female combat pilot in the US Armed Services. She flew an AH-1W SuperCobra attack helicopter in the 2003 invasion of Iraq and served two additional tours during Operation Iraqi Freedom. She was also the first naval aviator pilot in any branch of the military!

- **Jeanine Menze** was the first Black woman to earn a US Coast Guard aviator designation.

- **Major Shawna Rochelle Kimbrell** was the first Black American woman combat pilot in the United States Air Force. She flew an F-16 Fighting Falcon during Operation Northern Watch in Iraq.

- **Sherian Cadoria** was the first Black woman to earn the rank of brigadier general in the US Army.

- **Juanita Kidd Stout** was the first Black woman to serve on a state supreme court. She was named an associate justice of the Supreme Court of Pennsylvania in 1988.

- **Carol Moseley Braun** of Chicago was the first Black woman elected to the US Senate.

- **Carole Simpson** was the first Black woman to moderate a presidential debate. She moderated the second debate of the 1992 election.

- **Jacquelyn Barrett** was the first Black female sheriff in the United States. She was elected sheriff of Fulton County, Georgia, in November 1992.

- **Lillian Fishburne** was the first Black woman to reach the rank of rear admiral in the US Navy.

- In 2000, **Condoleezza Rice** became the first female US national security advisor of any race, and in 2005, she became the first Black American woman appointed US secretary of state.

- California representative **Karen Bass** was the first Black American woman to be elected speaker of a state house of representatives.

- **Susan Rice** was the first Black woman to become a United States ambassador to the United Nations.

MOLLY WILLIAMS:
Volunteer Eleven

Molly Williams became America's first female firefighter by working with New York's Oceanus Engine Company starting in 1818. Williams was the slave of a wealthy merchant who was a volunteer for the Oceanus Company. When influenza and cholera epidemics broke out, and many of the men were too ill to respond to calls, Williams stepped in. She became known as Volunteer 11 and was known to be as effective as any of the men in her fire station at fighting fires. Williams was enslaved by a man named John Aymar. Not much is known about her. We have an old illustration of Williams dressed in a calico dress with a scarf wrapped around her neck, pulling a pumper that held water to douse the flames in deep snow while White men are running away from the flames. What is known about Williams is that she and her husband bought their freedom from Aymar, though she continued to serve as his domestic servant, helping raise his eight children long after she was free. Her husband owned a successful tobacco shop, and the two of them had a son who served as a pastor in his church.

CATHAY WILLIAMS:
Buffalo Soldier

Cathay Williams was the first Black female to enlist in the US Army. She was born enslaved in 1844 in Independence, Missouri, to an enslaved woman and a freed man, which made her status that of a slave. During her adolescence, Williams worked as a house slave on the Johnson plantation. In 1866, she signed up for a three-year period of enlistment with the US Army as a Buffalo Soldier. The US was mired in the American Frontier Wars at the time, and Buffalo Soldiers were African American soldiers stationed in the Western US. Only a cousin and a friend knew of her enlistment. Both of them were stationed with the regiment she signed up to join. At the time of her enlistment, women were not allowed to serve, so she signed up under the assumed name "William Cathay." She served for two years until complications from smallpox led a military physician to discover that she was female. She was discharged from the army in 1868. After she was discharged from the army, Williams went on to work as a cook in New Mexico and later Colorado. She married, but it ended disastrously when her husband stole a team of horses and money from her. She had him arrested. It is believed she may have owned a boardinghouse. She worked as a seamstress for a time in Pueblo, Colorado. In 1875, a reporter from St. Louis heard rumors about a Black woman who had served in the army during the American Frontier Wars. He went to Colorado and interviewed Williams, and her story was published in the *St. Louis Daily Times* on January 2, 1876. In her old age, Williams suffered from complications of diabetes and neuralgia, and could only walk with a cane because her toes had been amputated. She applied for a disability pension, claiming her service in the army qualified her, but her disability claim was denied.

● ● ● ● ●

Black women were making surprising contributions to the military and to public service while the country was still shape-shifting from thirteen colonies into the union we know today. After the Civil War ended, many Black women moved north and west to escape the oppression in the South. They followed the expansion westward, pushing up against the boundaries of territories, and were pioneers who contributed to the wellbeing of often-untamed lands. These next women were pioneers in their own rights, brilliant trailblazers who were the first of their kind.

- "Stagecoach" **Mary Fields** became the first Black American woman to hold a star-route delivery contract with the United States Postal Service.

- **Carolyn R. Payton** became the first Black American and first woman appointed director of the US Peace Corps when she was appointed to the position by President Jimmy Carter.

- **Lisa P. Jackson** became the first Black American to be named administrator of the Environmental Protection Agency. She was appointed to the position by President Barack Obama.

- The first Black American woman four-star admiral was **Michelle J. Howard**. She was the first woman to rise to the rank of four-star admiral in the US Navy. Howard was also the first Black American woman to command a US Navy ship, the USS *Rushmore*. When she retired, she was serving as both commander of US Forces in Europe and as the commander of US Forces in Africa. She was the first woman to command operational forces for the US Military.

- **Lorna Mahlock** became the first Black American woman to hold the rank of brigadier general in the United States Marine Corps.

- **Loretta Lynch** was the first Black woman to become US attorney general.

- **Paulette Brown** became the first Black American woman president of the American Bar Association.

- **Carla Hayden** became the first woman and first Black American to be the librarian of Congress.

- **Andrea Jenkins** became the first openly transgender person of color elected to public office in the United States.

- **Stacey Abrams** of Georgia became the first Black American woman to be a major party nominee for state governor.

- **Ilhan Omar** became the first Somali American Muslim person to become a legislator when she was elected to Congress representing Minnesota.

Black women have proved their worth through their service to country and community. Often balancing the difficulties of home life with a successful career, they have excelled in military and public service. Let's not forget, these are fields that are dominated by White men. When asked to picture a brigadier general, chances are the last thing that comes to mind is a Black woman. But Black women can be brigadier generals too. We can be anything we set our minds to becoming.

• • • • •

The church has long been an important part of the Black community and has served as a source of consolation during difficult times. The church has also been a staging ground for organizing protests and has been active in the civil rights movement since its inception before slavery was even abolished. It is no wonder, then, that many of our bravest activists come from the flock of the church and serve the community with a spirit of defiance and dignity. Environmental historian and theologian **Rev. Dianne Glave** is adamant about bringing African Americans into the conversation concerning the history of the environment. American inspirational speaker, lawyer, New Thought spiritual teacher, author, life coach, and television personality **Iyanla Vanzant** utilizes courage to share her stories and encourage other women to live and walk a full life of spiritual and mental freedom.

The women in this section all have strong ties to their faith and have used it as a guidepost to lead them when faced with the challenge of making a difference in a world that often discards the contributions of Black women.

ESTHER IBANGA:
The Peacemaker

Esther Ibanga is a Nigerian pastor and dedicated community organizer for peace in conflict-ridden regions who has received the Niwano Peace Prize for her advocacy of peace and unity in Jos, Nigeria. She was born in 1961 in Kagbu, Nigeria, the seventh of ten children, eight of them girls. Both of her parents were very religious; her father was a policeman who won awards for his honesty and bravery, and her mother went on many mission trips as part of her involvement with her church. Ibanga earned a degree in business administration in 1983 from Ahmadu Bello University, and after serving the mandatory year in the National Youth Service Corps, she went to work for the Central Bank of Nigeria, where she eventually gained a position as a manager. She left the bank to become the first female church leader in the city of Jos, Nigeria, in 1995.

In 2010, Pastor Ibanga founded the Women Without Walls Initiative (WoWWI) in response to the constant state of crisis in Plateau State, Nigeria, since 2000. WoWWI is an NGO that includes Nigerian women from all walks of life and provides advocacy, training for women in building peace, mediation between warring parties, help for people displaced within Nigeria, assistance to the poor, empowerment of women and youth, and development projects in underprivileged areas to prevent grievances from sparking violent conflicts. Her hard work and dedication has helped to restore peace between Christian and Muslim communities in Jos North, a potentially volatile flashpoint. Her approach is to empower women, both inside and outside of Nigeria, to successfully strive to advance the status of women and children of all ethnicities, religions, and political leanings—to allow women to realize themselves as "natural agents of change."

Pastor Ibanga was the leader of a march in February
2010 to the Jos Government House in protest of the
Dogon Nahawa ethno-religious crisis, in which many lives,
including those of women and children, had been lost; more
than 100,000 women, all dressed in black, participated.
When 276 teenage girls were kidnapped by Boko Haram
terrorists from their school in Chibok, Nigeria, WoWWI
joined in the Bring Back Our Girls campaign with other
women leaders. Rallies crossing religious and cultural lines
were held to demand that the government expedite the
girls' release. Pastor Ibanga continues to campaign for the
freeing of the 113 girls who are still held captive, and speaks
internationally on the issue.

KATY FERGUSON:
Earth Angel

Born a slave in 1779, Catherine Ferguson accompanied
her mistress to church on Sundays until she was freed at
sixteen by a White woman benefactor who paid $200 for
Ferguson's emancipation. Two years later, she married;
by the time she was twenty, her husband and two infant
children were dead. Ferguson, a fantastic baker, made
wedding cakes and other delicacies to support herself.
On the way to market to sell her baked goods, she would
see dozens of poor children and orphans who pulled at
the strings of her heart. The indomitable Ferguson started
teaching these waifs church classes in her home on what is
now Warren Street in Manhattan, until a Dr. Mason lent her
church basement in 1814. This is believed to be the origin of

what we now call Sunday school. Ferguson's classes were so popular that droves of poor Black and White children came to learn. Soon, many young, unwed mothers started showing up, too, who she took home to care for and teach them self-reliance. Ferguson died of cholera in 1854, but her work carried on in the Katy Ferguson Home for unwed mothers, where kindness, good works, and good learning are the helping hands to a better life.

SOUL SISTERS

Sister Rosetta Tharpe was a pioneering guitarist and singer who became known as the "godmother of rock and roll" and the "original soul sister." She was born in 1915 in Cotton Plant, Arkansas. Her mother was a singer and mandolin player who performed at her local church. Sister Tharpe proved herself to be a prodigy and picked up the guitar at the age of four. By the age of six she was touring the South with a traveling evangelical troupe that included her mother. At the age of twenty-three, she recorded her first albums with Decca Records. Her first recordings, which were a mix of gospel and what would later be known as rock and roll music, were instant hits. Sister Tharpe was a pioneer in her guitar technique, which featured heavy distortion. She was the first great gospel recording artist and brought gospel music into the mainstream. She also influenced several musicians, including Elvis Presley, Eric Clapton, Chuck Berry, Little Richard, and Carl Perkins. Sister Tharpe continued recording and traveling on tour, gaining a worldwide following. She died in 1973 at the age of fifty-eight. Sister Tharpe was inducted into the Rock and Roll Hall of Fame as an early influence in 2018.

Sister Gertrude Morgan was an American artist, musician, poet, and preacher. She was born in 1900 in LaFayette, Alabama. Sister Morgan left school before she completed the third grade. Sometime around 1917 her family moved to Columbus, Georgia, where she worked as a servant and a nursemaid. In 1939, she moved to New Orleans, Louisiana, where she lived until her death. Throughout her life, Sister Morgan received many revelations from God. In 1956, God urged her to begin painting. Her paintings depicted religious subjects. Sister Morgan was a street preacher, and she used both music and her artwork in her sermons. Around 1960, Sister Morgan met an art dealer while preaching on the street. He invited her to his gallery to perform and display her work, and her popularity took off. She worked with whatever material was available to her, including cardboard, window shades, Styrofoam trays, plastic utensils, jelly glasses, blocks of wood, her guitar case, and the back of a "For Sale" sign that a real estate agent placed outside her home. She began exhibiting her work at galleries all around the country. Sister Morgan died in 1980.

Yolanda Adams is an American gospel singer, record producer, actress, author, and radio show host. She was born in Houston, Texas, in 1961. She earned a degree in radio/television broadcasting from Texas Southern University and went to work as a teacher after college. Adams first gained attention as a singer with Houston's

Southeast Inspirational Choir, where she was a lead singer. In 1982, the choir released a single called "For My Liberty" that featured her as the vocalist. Her first mainstream breakthrough came with the release of Mountain High... Valley Low in 1999. The album won a Grammy award and went double platinum. Adams went on to win four more Grammy Awards, five BET Awards, six NAACP Image Awards, six Soul Train Music Awards, two BMI Awards, and sixteen Stellar Awards. She made history as the first gospel musician to win an American Music Award. In 2009, she was named Billboard magazine's top-selling gospel artist from 1999-2009. In 2016, President Barack Obama presented her with the Presidential Lifetime Achievement Award for her volunteer work. In 2017, she was inducted into the Gospel Hall of Fame. She hosted a radio program, The Yolanda Adams Morning Show, from 2007-2016. In 2010, she published her book Points of Power. The title comes from one of the segments on her radio program. Adams was the spokesperson for Operation Rebound, a program sponsored by FILA Corporation that helped inner-city schoolchildren. She said, "I truly believe that my songs bring the answers and the solutions, as opposed to just talking about the problems. My music at its core is joyful."

FIRST IN FAITH

Black women of faith have come far in their quest to shape their communities and reshape the world. The following women were pioneers in their churches and achieved accomplishments that no one before them ever had. They have reshaped the paradigm of belief systems and giving spirited leadership to their congregations.

- The first Black woman to be ordained as an Episcopal priest was **Pauli Murray**. She was also the first woman to receive a PhD in juridical science from Yale Law School.

- The first Black American woman ordained by the Lutheran Church in America, the largest of three denominations that later combined to form the Evangelical Lutheran Church in America, was **Earlean Miller**.

- **Barbara Clementine Harris** was the first Black woman and the first woman of any race to be ordained as a bishop in the Anglican Communion (Episcopal Church).

- **Merle Kodo Boyd** was the first Black American woman to receive Dharma transmission in Zen Buddhism, meaning she was recognized as capable of being a successor in the religion's lineage.

- **Alysa Stanton** was the first Black American female rabbi. In 2009, Rabbi Stanton became the first Black American rabbi to lead a majority-White congregation.

● ● ● ● ●

Black women stand out in the church, in the military, and in government service. The ties that bind them to service are laced tightly, and you can see their dedication to the Black community in their life's work. These women have built schools, led revolts, and revolutionized the way Black women choose to be seen in the public sphere. All three of these areas, church, military, and government service, are male-dominated fields. It is unusual for any woman to make a difference in these arenas, but these ladies stepped up and proved themselves to be warriors.

Conclusion: But Wait, There's So Much More

And Now the End Is Here

We hope you've enjoyed learning about all the awesome Black women we've featured. Researching their biographies for this project was a real joy, and definitely an eye-opener. We've wracked our heads trying to find the most relevant categories to give you a good overview of how Black women have historically shaped, and are presently shaping, the world, but we know there's so much more that we couldn't cover in a single volume. It is important to remember, too, that there's a historical gap that lasts about four hundred years when many Black women were not actively making history because they were enslaved. The accomplishments of these women and their potential are lost to this blank spot in history. The history of Black women in America is still largely being written. New discoveries about our shared past are still being made today. Who knows what artifacts are lying undisturbed in someone's attic. There's a good chance that another novel like *Our Nig* by Harriet Wilson is waiting to be found and cherished for the insight it gives us into our collective pasts.

We have come a long way since the days of slavery, but we still have a long way to go toward ensuring that every Black woman has the opportunity to meet their potential. Hopefully, reading about the women in this book has given you a new appreciation for awesome Black women and a fraction of their accomplishments.

To Learn More:

The National Archives for Black Women's History is the largest repository solely dedicated to the collection and preservation of material relating to African American women. The collection includes correspondence, photographs, and speeches. For further information, please contact 202-673-2402, or for more information, see its page in the Library of Congress web site: loc.gov/folklife/civilrights/survey/view_repository.php?rep_id=1667

WHO ARE YOUR AWESOME WOMEN?

Dear Reader,

This book almost never made it to the printer because we kept finding more and more fascinating females deserving to be honored in the annals of history. We would love to have a follow-up volume detailing the lives and times of more role models. We invite you to email, tweet, or send a note with your nomination of your Awesome Women. We would love to hear from you about this and continue the celebration of these "great unknowns" who didn't make it into the history books UNTIL NOW!

Below is a simple nomination form, and we would love to credit you, so please include your contact information. Thanks for your participation - you are pretty awesome, yourself!

xoxo

Becca and M.J.

- - - - - - - - - - - - - - - - - - - -

I Nominate the Following Awesome Woman:

_____

_____

_____

_____

_____

Mango Publishing 2850 Douglas Road
4th Floor, Coral Gables, Florida 33134

Twitter: @MangoPublishing
Email: support@mangopublishinggroup.com

About the Authors

Becca Anderson comes from a long line of preachers and teachers from Ohio and Kentucky. The teacher side of her family led her to become a woman's studies scholar and the author of The Book of Awesome Women. An avid collector of meditations, prayers, and blessings, she helps run a "Gratitude and Grace Circle" virtual circle that meets weekly. In non-pandemic times, she gives gratitude workshops at churches and bookstores in the San Francisco Bay Area, where she currently resides. Becca Anderson credits her spiritual practice with helping her recover from cancer and wants to share this healing wisdom with anyone who is facing difficulty in their life.

Born in Port-au-Prince, **M.J. Fievre**, BS Ed, is a long-time educator and writer. M.J. earned a bachelor's degree in education from Barry University. A seasoned K–12 teacher, she spent much time building up her students, helping them feel comfortable in their own skin, and affirming their identities. She has taught creative writing workshops to children at the O, Miami Poetry Festival and the Miami Art Museum, as well as in various schools in Santa Cruz de la Sierra (Bolivia), Port-au-Prince (Haiti), and South Florida. As the ReadCaribbean program coordinator for the prestigious Miami Book Fair, M.J. also directs and produces the children's cultural show *Taptap Krik? Krak!*

Mango Publishing, established in 2014, publishes an eclectic list of books by diverse authors—both new and established voices—on topics ranging from business, personal growth, women's empowerment, LGBTQ studies, health, and spirituality to history, popular culture, time management, decluttering, lifestyle, mental wellness, aging, and sustainable living. We were recently named 2019 *and* 2020's #1 fastest-growing independent publisher by *Publishers Weekly*. Our success is driven by our main goal, which is to publish high-quality books that will entertain readers as well as make a positive difference in their lives.

Our readers are our most important resource; we value your input, suggestions, and ideas. We'd love to hear from you—after all, we are publishing books for you!

Please stay in touch with us and follow us at:

Facebook: Mango Publishing
Twitter: @MangoPublishing
Instagram: @MangoPublishing
LinkedIn: Mango Publishing
Pinterest: Mango Publishing
Newsletter: mangopublishinggroup.com/newsletter

Join us on Mango's journey to reinvent publishing, one book at a time.